To my wonderful and lively grandchildren,

Elayna and Enzo,

Whose company always helps to keep me young,

active and entertained.

The Kings & Queens of England & Britain.

Introduction.

Not many nations can boast of having had such a long succession of Kings and Queens than England can. Once the last Roman legion had left, the British Isles became fair game for the raiders from across the sea, Germanic tribes who saw an opportunity. They'd already tested the defences even before the Romans withdrew, but soon they viewed England as something they might actually conquer and keep. Ultimately, the Saxons won the contest and so began the list of names of those who styled themselves as King or Queen. Having one person as supreme leader of a tribe or nation was considered to be the right thing to do, the natural order of things, and it was considered equally natural for that person's heirs to continue the line, passing the mantle of leadership and rule onto the next one in the hope it would maintain order and stability. Few could have imagined at the time just how far that mantle would have passed. The houses who took control may have changed, but the title, and all that it meant, didn't. Over time, the way the Kings and Queens ruled did change. As society changed through technology, civil wars, plague and the growing awareness of some people concerning their rights and hoped for freedom, so too did the monarchy realise, eventually, that perhaps they too needed to change the way they led. The transition from the divine right of Kings to a constitutional monarchy was slow and painful.

Much blood would have to be spilt before one side or the other prevailed, leaving the nation, and people, very different. It was the civil war between King and parliament in the seventeenth century which temporarily saw the abolition of the role of King, though most people wanted it to be restored at the first opportunity. Yet, the Kings and Queens who followed realised they had to tread more carefully, more so after the Glorious Revolution. With greater enlightenment, scientific discoveries and the general pursuit of knowledge, people wanted more of a say in how they were ruled, desired more of a role than just the traditional subject who was told what to do. Then came empire with its wave of patriotic fervour and imperialistic sense of bringing justice and order to the world. For many, the empire was something wonderful, almost preordained by God which was the instrument by which He would work through them to make the world a better place. However, this imperialism would be tested on several occasions and found wanting. Not far into the twentieth century, even humble farmers were able to successfully challenge all the might the empire could throw at them. The empire won, but it showed its competitors just how flawed it really was. So, once the empire did finally clash with its main rival, Germany, what followed were two brutal world wars of annihilation, where each sought domination over the other, where each threw everything they had into forcing the other's defeat. The British Empire, assisted by her allies, won both contests, but the cost of success ruined her. After World War Two, the empire was broke and had to go cap in hand to the United States for money just to make ends meet, the same United States which had successfully fought Britain for her independence. The Commonwealth had followed empire, but one by one the individual nations desired independence and the right to rule themselves. Britain had once literally ruled the waves, but the growth of other superpowers, thanks mostly to the world wars, had given that title to somebody else, and because the empire's colonies and interests were overseas, spread across the globe, it could no longer send one of her gunboats to some distant corner of empire to sort the locals out. Economic decline and social unrest took their toll, and, with the breakup of her imperial structure, many must have believed the end was in sight. But, despite all the incredible social and political storms that came her way, Britain still retained her monarchy. It came out of the fire of war a much different creature than when it entered, far more aware of its fragile nature, but also far more aware of what the monarchy stood for in the modern world.

The path of the British monarchy has been a very turbulent and bloody one. It has seen the rise of a great maritime nation which then blossomed into empire whilst at the same time keeping her enemies and competitors at bay. It has seen near misses too, times when events looked as if they would overtake the Royal house and leave it destroyed in favour of a republic, or worse, but it always survived, ready to pass on the crown to the next one in line. This is the story of that line of monarchs who called themselves King or Queen of England and Britain.

I hope you will forgive me for not including all the details about all the monarchs, as to do so would have meant the book would be ten times as long, and probably would have been incredibly boring in places too. Instead, the verses I've written include some of the more interesting facts about them. Also, some monarchs might appear to have more verses than others. This is because in some reigns many momentous events took place, whilst in others there were less. For example, George V had to rule during the Great War and the Great Depression, whilst also seeing the empire begin to fragment, or at least see the first cracks. Conversely, Edward VI, the young boy king, wasn't alive that long and therefore not so much happened in his reign. However, if I haven't done your favourite King or Queen justice, then I apologise again. I've also included King Alfred in the book as well. Although he was never the King of all England, I feel his presence in the book is necessary as his reign is both memorable and important to the story. What's more, I hope that what I've included will encourage your interest in the history of

Britain, that it will fire your enthusiasm to find out more. After all, there aren't that many nations in this modern world whose history is so fascinating and interesting.

Index.

(Saxons)

Alfred – P.16

Athelstan – P.23

Edmund – P.27

Eadred – P.30

Eadwig – P.33

Edgar – P.36

Edward The Martyr – P.38

Aethelred II (The Unready) – P.42

(Vikings)

Cnut (The Great) – P.49

Harold I (Harefoot) – P.59

Harthacanut – P.63

(Saxons)

Edward The Confessor – P.70

Harold II – P.80

(Normans)

William The Conqueror – P.90

William II (Rufus) – P.98

Henry I – P.104

Stephen – P.114

(The House of Plantagenet)

Henry II – P.122

Richard I (The Lion heart) – P.130

John – P.145

Henry III – P.152

Edward I – P.158

Edward II – P.164

Edward III – P.170

Richard II – P.178

(House of Lancaster)

Henry IV – P.186

Henry V – P.193

Henry VI – P.198

(The House of York)

Edward IV – P.208

Edward V – P.215

Richard III – P.219

(The Tudors)

Henry VII – P.226

Henry VIII – P.236

Edward VI – P.269

Mary I – P.278

Elizabeth I – P.290

(The Stuarts)

James I – P.333

Charles I – P.340

(The Commonwealth)

Oliver Cromwell

(Lord Protector) – P.366

(The Restoration)

Charles II – P.382

James II – P.394

William III & Mary II – P.402

Anne – P.410

(The House of Hanover)

George I – P.419

George II – P.426

George III – P.437

George IV – P.460

William IV – P.466

Victoria – P.471

(The House of Saxe Coburg-Gotha/Windsor)

Edward VII – P.496

George V – P.506

Edward VIII – P.524

George VI – P.530

Elizabeth II – P.544

Charles III – P.559

The Saxons

Interesting fact:

In the later Roman period, the name 'Saxon' was used to describe coastal raiders from the Germanic tribes from across the sea.

Since the Romans left in four hundred and ten,
England had seen many great men,
Trying to rule and do their best,
Though often at war and often oppressed.

The Britons tried to stem the flow,
Of tribes which invaded and tried to show,
That the Britons would have to bend the knee,
To invaders who came from across the sea.

The Saxons eventually took control,
Giving England a different soul,
Removing the last of the ancient ways,
As England entered a different phase.

For centuries, separate kingdoms existed,
By Saxon Kings who each insisted,
There piece of land was unlike the others,
Even though they all were Saxon brothers.

Wessex became a mighty state,
From which would stem England's fate.
From her came laws and the shire,
Where a dream of England would aspire.

Yet Saxon England remained divided,
With its future rule almost decided,
When Viking forces began attacking,
Their warriors pillaging and ransacking.

The first of the raids was in seven ninety-three,
The first in a line of a killing spree,
Which left the Saxons in mortal fear,
Of attacks which suddenly might appear.

On and off the raids came and went,
Full of fury and then they were spent,
With the Vikings taking their plunder and slaves,
Leaving more Saxons to be put in their graves.

Subsequent Saxon Kings did their best,
To rise to the challenge and pass the test,
Of trying to rule and protect each subject,
Who, to the Viking, was a valuable object.

King Alfred
(871 – 899 AD)

Interesting fact:

Alfred encouraged learning, and he was so keen to help people become better educated, that he proposed teaching should be conducted using English instead of the traditional Latin.

A man rose to power who broke the chain,
Of Saxon oppression from the fierce Dane,
The youngest son to a noble line,
Destiny would a great task assign.

Ethelbald, Ethelberht and Ethelred,
His brothers who'd ruled, each in their stead,
Had similar problems seen and faced,
And Alfred's mind would need to be braced.

For he was to be the very next,
To rule the kingdom of Wessex,
The southern lands and tranquil shires,
Set ablaze by Viking fires.

But as the King, Alfred showed,
How much reform to him was owed,
As he did his best to try to improve,
Ways of ruling and corruption remove.

Known for his intellect and mercy too,
His reputation as King quickly grew,
Fair, just and highly respected,
The kingdom of Wessex was well directed.

But the Viking menace had not gone away,
The fear of attack filling each day,
And defeat at their hands made him agree,
To pay them with silver to keep his lands free.

Yet the Danes came back after a while,
Full of longing, ambition and guile,
Taking Wareham in Dorset by storm,
Though Alfred's force at Wareham would swarm.

Forced to agree to talks and a truce,
The Danes agreed to no further abuse,
Then broke the truce to plunder some more,
Shocking the west country to the core.

Truce followed war and vice versa,
As Danes withdrew to bases in Mercia,
Until they attacked and forced Alfred to flee,
To a Somerset marsh at Athelney.

From here, the King was able to make,
A resistance for all of England's sake,
For the other kingdoms had fallen already,
While Alfred's commitment was ever steady.

Some say he wondered what to do in the marsh,
Where conditions were always basic and harsh,
Hiding away in a place damp and cold,
Planning that victory might unfold.

Legends arose of a task being given,
To watch some cakes and him being driven,
Away because some cakes were burnt,
An old lady moaning, and his lesson learnt.

But Alfred's patience finally paid,
As all the while his plans were laid,
To have the forces of Wessex assemble,
That might make the Viking warriors tremble.

At Eddington, Alfred defeated them all,
Saw the mask of invincibility fall,
Forcing the Danes to agree to a peace,
Which saw his kingdom's longed for release.

The Viking domains were restricted,
To northern lands and there constricted,
To what would be known as the Danelaw,
A culture from which generations would draw.

Yet the Viking lust for war and treasure,
The way they'd find their enemy's measure,
Had forced them into further attacks,
With Alfred having to face the facts.

Despite his efforts to find a peace,
Alfred's kingdom found no release,
From Viking bands and armies which sought,
To conquer, plunder and leave people distraught.

But Alfred proved he was their match,
Knowing when and where to dispatch,
His Saxon forces to stem the tide,
To try and force the threat aside.

And all the while he created a code,
Of laws from which his justice flowed,
Also saying that English be used,
In schools as Latin left many confused.

But in eight ninety-nine, after so much,
After he'd given his own special touch,
Alfred died and left it to those,
Born and bred to wear a King's clothes.

Subsequent Kings would have to deal,
With Viking raiders who'd try to steal,
People, land, and Saxon wealth,
The ships arriving with skill and stealth.

Alfred reformed much in his realm,
So that future foes could not overwhelm,
Saxon forces with relative ease,
Or invade and pillage as they please.

When Alfred died in eight ninety-nine,
He left the Kings who were next in line,
A Saxon nation which was strong and wealthy,
Its army reformed, its economy healthy.

What followed would be an incredible thing,
A line of monarchs who would bring,
Glory, tragedy, war and fame,
Majesty, conquest riches and shame.

Athelstan
(925-939)

Interesting fact:

Athelstan never married, but he successfully arranged marriages for his sisters to several continental European monarchs.

The grandson of King Alfred the Great,
His reign would bring about a state,
Which all of Europe would fear and admire,
A state to which most would truly aspire.

As Mercia's King he was embraced,
But he wasn't to all of England's taste,
So, when the throne of Wessex was free,
The nobles of Wessex would not bend the knee.

But Athelstan triumphed, and soon took the throne,
Ruling both Mercia and Wessex alone,
Forging from both a large Saxon home,
The biggest since the presence of Rome.

Though he knew the Vikings still had hold,
Of the kingdom of York and still were bold,
Always there as a constant threat,
Their reputation as invaders set.

Athelstan knew that he must prove,
His status as warrior and also remove,
The Viking threat once and for all,
The threat of invasion to forestall.

This he did and so England saw,
Something not seen since Rome's withdraw,
A unified nation under one lord,
A king of justice and the sword.

The Saxon kingdom had never seen,
A kingdom so large or ever been,
Ruled with such justice and piety too,
As Athelstan's power and influence grew.

He invaded Scotland and forced them to kneel,
Bringing a possible threat to heel,
And he even encouraged the Welsh to accept,
His over lordship that peace might be kept.

The nations of respected his reign,
With many seeking a link to attain,
Through marriage to his royal house,
Alliances made by seeking a spouse.

For too short a time, Athelstan ruled,
During which time all England was schooled,
In the ways of piety, law and peace,
Which many feared, with his death, would cease.

He was the first to unite all the lands,
To make a whole England from warring bands.
England was young but still their home,
No longer a home to the legions of Rome.

Edmund
(939-946)

Interesting fact:

Edmund was keen to reform the legal system, and one of his legal codes deals with theft and cattle rustling. Local communities were required, by law, to track down the offenders and bring them in, dead or alive!

Once Athelstan died, the crown would go,
To his half-brothers who'd have to show,
If they were both up to the role,
Of keeping the kingdom safe and whole.

Edmund was first to have the chance,
Either to fail or even enhance,
The kingdom which his half-brother built,
Or would he let the legacy wilt.

With the old king dead, the Vikings moved,
To regaining the north, which was approved,
By those in York whose loyalty lay,
With Viking rule and the Danish way.

The Viking king of Dublin was picked,
As king of York who would inflict,
A collapse of Saxon rule in the north,
Bringing years of bloody warfare forth.

Olaf was the Viking chief,
Who gave the Danes in the north relief,
From Saxon rule to which they objected,
Wanting the old rule they respected.

When Olaf died in nine forty-one,
Edmund thought the troubles were done,
And the northern lands were soon retaken,
But thoughts of stability were mistaken.

For Edmund died and the north returned,
To Viking rule to which people yearned,
So, then king Eadred would have to try,
His skills as a ruler to apply.

Eadred
(946-955)

Interesting fact:

Like with all Saxon Kings, there was no fixed capital city, and the King and his court would travel across the country from one of his estates to another. There was also no central treasury, but the King carried his religious relics wherever he went.

For several long years, Eadred would strive,
To keep the thought of an England alive,
Leading his army to face the foe,
To try and deliver the knockout blow.

The lands and people would suffer most,
As Viking and Saxon warrior host,
Went through the north to kill each other,
With death for each father, son or brother.

But as the war continued each year,
Without a victory coming near,
The Northumbrians finally played their hand,
Making a choice to make a stand.

Eric Bloodaxe was the Viking they'd drive,
From the northern lands that it might thrive,
Instead of having two armies fighting,
Across the lands and destruction inviting.

Once the Viking King had withdrawn,
Once the cycle of warfare was torn,
The north, at last, had to admit,
That to Eadred they'd have to submit.

After years of turmoil, war and division,
When Saxon and Viking were in collision,
England was one and united once more,
Ruled by one king just as before.

Bloody war had plagued and spoiled,
The lands on which the people toiled,
But Danes in the north showed disdain,
For Saxon rule and fought for their gain.

Eadwig
(955-959)

Interesting fact:

Eadwig was only fifteen when he became King, and one of the first things he did was to promote his closest friends to high office, something which made the 'Old Guard' angry and led to division and plots.

The son of Edmund, he took the crown,
When his father was cut down,
In defence of his lands on campaign,
Bringing an end to his own reign.

Still a young man, Eadwig was told,
His thoughts for the crown he'd have to hold,
As he was too young and would have to wait,
While uncle Eadred ruled the state.

But Eadred died when he was quite young,
So, the mantle of King had to be hung,
Upon the shoulders of the boy in his teens,
And he'd learn to rule by any means.

At just fifteen when he gained the throne,
He issued charters which set the tone,
For a reign in which he wanted to prove,
The old guard and old ways he sought to remove.

The Abbot of Glastonbury was exiled,
Making Eadwig feared and reviled,
As he sought to build his power base,
To give all England a brand-new face.

Yet the Abbot, in time, retaliated,
When he told the King he'd calculated,
Eadwig's bride was too closely related,
So, annulment was quickly activated.

Then northern troubles soon provided,
A reason why England should be divided.
Edgar, his brother, was allowed to govern,
Lands north of the Thames, with Eadwig the southern.

But this arrangement didn't last very long,
Didn't have time to be felt right or wrong,
As in nine fifty-nine Eadwig was dead,
So, Edgar was crowned King of England instead.

Edgar
(959-975)

Interesting fact:

Supporting religious reform, under Edgar there was an increase in literature and art, but Monasteries aggressively gained more lands, and this caused much anger and frustration among many of the people.

The youngest son of King Edmund the first,
Though young he wasn't too unversed,
In political ways and how to act,
Aware that a king needed guile and tact.

The Abbot of Glastonbury was recalled,
And the Abbot was installed,
As Archbishop of Canterbury and his aide,
With whom he sought counsel, wisdom and prayed.

Though young, much under Edgar was achieved,
As people in England saw and believed,
That here was a king who had brought,
Stability, piety which most of them sought.

Known as Edgar the Peaceful to most,
A time of peace is what England could boast,
And his great coronation he had in Bath,
Inspired most monarchs to follow its path.

Edward The Martyr (975-978)

Interesting fact:

Although he was the eldest son of Edgar, he was not acknowledged as heir to the throne. It is believed that the Dowager Queen paid assassins to murder him.

Edgar's son, but not thought of as heir,
When he was crowned some thought it unfair,
That the bishops who crowned him went too far,
Crowning him for their own rising star.

For many believed Ethelred, his half-brother,
Though younger, would be best placed than the other,
And Edward, if the bishops confessed,
Had not, by his father, for king been blessed.

So, division was followed by serious plotting,
With Edward's position teetering, rotting.
As plans for civil war were laid,
Plans for a murder were soon to be made.

As Edward position as king was weak,
Saxon nobles would try to seek,
An attack on the strong Benedictine church,
Its position and character to besmirch.

King Edgar had made the church too strong,
Which some Saxon nobles thought was wrong,
So, whilst Edward faced potential dissent,
The nobles moved to the church's lament.

Benedictine monasteries were dispossessed,
Their power and influence soon suppressed,
With Edward seemingly unable to act,
As the persecution by the nobles was backed.

Civil war was further evaded,
When certain nobles were persuaded,
To murder young Edward whilst in the south,
Forever to silence the King's noble mouth.

At Corfe, in Dorset, with daring and luck,
The assassins waited and there they struck,
Leaving young Edward mortally slain,
While those at fault would not shift the blame.

At Wareham in Dorset, his body was placed,
The body prepared and buried in haste,
With the Dowager Queen, Ethelred's mother,
Suspected of murdering Ethelred's brother.

Edward was seen as not very strong,
Perhaps because his reign wasn't long,
But though some thought he was a nonstarter,
He soon acquired the title of Martyr.

Aethelred II (The Unready) (978-1016)

Interesting fact:

The name 'Unready' was something which was added to Aethelred's name in the twelfth century, and it was probably never used by anyone of his time.

He was only twelve when he succeeded,
To the throne, but advice was needed,
To help him rule as king and Lord,
As mistakes a king could ill afford.

Being so young, it was decided,
He would need help and to be guided,
In making decisions for what was best,
That matters of state might be addressed.

His name in old English means 'well advised',
But some on his council were despised,
So, he was known and soon became,
'Unready' as people played on the name.

For England was at war yet again,
Having to face more raids by the Dane,
Whose raids became frequent and much worse,
Like a constant sore, a constant curse.

A Saxon army had to be sent,
To face the Viking and it was meant,
To defeat the foe and send them packing,
But all was lost with the Vikings attacking.

Ethelred and his advisors were shocked,
With the thought of defeat and being locked,
In a bitter war on English soil,
Aware how the Danes would ravage and spoil.

But his council, his Witan, had the idea,
Of ending the fighting, removing all fear,
Advising the King to pay a large fee,
A Danegeld which would keep England free.

For years both sides lived in peace,
With many believing it wouldn't cease,
But in ten 0-two, Ethelred made,
An attack on the Danes, the peace betrayed.

Completely taken by surprise,
Victims couldn't believe their eyes,
As Saxons slaughtered each Dane they found,
Their blood awash on English ground.

News of the slaughter soon got out,
And Danes rose up with a mighty shout,
For revenge for those who'd died they feared,
Being led by their king, Sweyn Forkbeard.

Yet it took some years before the Danes acted,
Their plans delayed and protracted,
Until they landed in ten-thirteen,
A more determined army few had seen.

England, once more, had been invaded,
But Ethelred acted and quickly evaded,
The Viking, force escaping abroad,
Which showed how he by the foe was awed.

Sweyn was now the king of the land,
Though his tenure as king wouldn't stand,
For within two years Sweyn was dead,
So, Ethelred returned as England's head.

The war with the Danes still went on,
But Forkbeard's threat now was gone,
Yet Cnut, his son, still carried the flame,
For war and revenge in the Vikings name.

Ethelred with his son fought hard,
That Viking success might be barred.
At last, the invading force was defeated,
And Cnut, for a while, to Denmark retreated.

In all his thirty-seven years of ruling,
Of his learning to lead and political schooling,
England's populace, trade and wealth expanded,
So, it's unfair with 'unready' he is branded.

His conflicts with the Danes were the root,
Of disruption in England which was acute.
Yet for law-and-order Ethelred cared,
And under his law few transgressors were spared.

Edmund, his son would take his place,
But within a few months death would embrace,
The brave young king, who wouldn't yield,
And was called 'Ironside' on the battlefield.

Ethelred's rule was seen by most,
As that which the Saxon could clearly boast,
For its justice, wealth and its strength,
But also, for its incredible length.

Despite the invasions and the war,
The reign of Ethelred was steeped in law,
Who used a council called Witan,
To rule the land and every man.

The Vikings

Interesting fact:

It is possible that global temperatures had increased very slightly around this time, but enough for the northern nations and tribes across the North Sea to lose large parts of their lands, causing them to sail in search of new lands and wealth in the south.

Cnut (The Great) (1016-1035)

Interesting fact:

So powerful and influential was he after his victories in Norway and Sweden, that Cnut was able to attend the coronation of the Holy Roman Emperor, soon after declaring himself King of all England, Denmark, Norway and some of the Swedes.

The Vikings still had wounded pride,
From when the Saxon king had tried,
To kill all Vikings in his domain,
That he might Viking growth contain.

For a while it worked, and Saxon strength,
Within all England grew at length,
With the Viking people killed or fled,
Their hopes of lands in England dead.

But Vikings under Sweyn Forkbeard,
Cnut's own father who was feared,
Successfully launched his own attack,
With much of the losses taken back.

Forkbeard forced a Saxon retreat,
With even Londoners having to greet,
Viking forces marching into the city,
As England fell to Sweyn's mercy and pity.

But Forkbeard's rule didn't last very long,
Just a few weeks which helped along,
Saxon resurgence, and they, in turn,
Returned to fight and made Vikings burn.

Yet the Viking king, Cnut, had planned,
An invasion force which was manned,
By Vikings from across his realm,
Who, for vengeance, donned the helm.

Perhaps ten thousand men or more,
Would land upon the Wessex shore,
Sailing up the river Frome,
To sack and burn each Saxon home.

Their wrath was fierce and so intense,
It shook the Saxon's own defence,
As the Vikings left a trail of destruction,
As part of Saxon England's reduction.

Ethelred sent his eldest son,
Believing he'd do what had to be done,
With Edmund Ironside leading the way,
At the head of the Saxons into the fray.

By ten-fifteen, Wessex was lost,
The kingdom submitting at great cost,
Then one of the Mercian earls defected,
Leaving part of the kingdom unprotected.

So many people, peasant or Lord,
Had Viking blood and were in accord,
With what Cnut's was trying to do,
So joined the cause they felt to be true.

The Danes pushed on and were soon in the north,
Subduing the Saxons as they went forth,
And though Edmund Ironside did his best,
It seemed his forces were not up to the test.

Edmund was forced to retreat once more,
To within London's walls to there restore,
His forces and strength that he might return,
To fighting the foe, his main concern.

But in ten-sixteen the pressure grew,
When Ethelred died and Edmund knew,
That he would have to rule and fight,
For his rights and always be in sight.

The Danes marched south with hopes to ensnare,
Edmund in London to be caught in his lair,
But Edmund left, so the trap was evaded,
Though the city itself was soon blockaded.

Escaping to Wessex, he hoped to raise,
An army and march without further delays,
Back to the fight and destroy the root,
The source of his woe, the Viking Cnut.

The Saxons gave as good as they got,
Trying to stem the tide and the rot.
Through force and tactics Edmund achieved,
What many on both sides hadn't perceived.

Though wounded, he forced Cnut to agree,
To a deal which kept Saxon lands free,
Where Cnut and Edmund duly signed,
A treaty that war might be confined.

North of the Thames would belong to the Dane,
Whilst London and the south would remain,
Under Edmund that Saxon ways might survive,
That a Saxon kingdom might stay alive.

It was also agreed upon Edmund's demise,
That Cnut as sole ruler of all would arise,
So, suspicion arose when shortly later,
Edmund died and Cnut's strength was greater.

As king of England, Cnut moved fast,
To ensure his rule would thrive and last,
By having opposing nobles purged,
While Saxon supporters then emerged.

This was followed by a suitable marriage,
Which few, if any, dared disparage,
To Emma, Ethelred's widowed Queen,
A move which most had not foreseen.

With his power base made more secure,
Feeling his reign might really endure,
Cnut raised a tax to help him pay,
For the army that needed dispersing away.

Then in ten-eighteen, Cnut acquired,
The Danish throne which he'd desired,
Which gave more strength to his power base,
A grander look to an imperial face.

For Cnut was doing his best to build,
A northern empire which would be filled,
With Saxon and Viking people who,
Living as one, the economy grew.

He saw that Danes and Saxons had,
Fought in the past and relations were bad,
But he also knew that when compared,
Their cultures and customs were often shared.

He sought to bring both races together,
Through common ties to see if whether,
As a people, united, they'd achieve,
Rewards of peace if they'd only believe.

Ten years later, in ten twenty-eight,
After years of warfare, blood and hate,
Cnut won the throne of Norway as well,
Which saw his reputation swell.

With such power, even Scotland admitted,
To Cnut's strength all must be submitted,
Though his hold on the Scots was always weak,
With the chance of holding Scotland bleak.

His influence in Ireland also improved,
With trade by both duly approved,
As the king of England had resolved,
In ties of trade to be involved.

Cnut's reputation was so great,
He was recognised by each Christian state,
As a king to be given friendship, respect,
Whose good will and favour they'd best not neglect.

English, Norwegians, Danes and Swedes,
All, in their way, were part of the seeds,
Which grew an empire and forged a peace,
But this North Sea Empire would fail and cease.

For a time, there existed a wonderful dream,

An empire, united, or so it would seem.

Cnut and Emma, ruling and married,

Their royal titles earned and carried.

Harold I (Harefoot) (1035-1040)

Interesting fact:

His name 'Harefoot' is first seen in the twelfth century and according to some medieval writers it meant that he was considered 'fleet of foot', fast.

When Cnut died in ten thirty-five,
Harold's reign would soon derive,
Trouble with his brother, who said,
The crown was rightfully his instead.

Harthacnut was Harold's half-brother,
Of the same father but different mother,
With Harthacnut fighting across the sea,
Against the Danes who fought to be free.

Before his departure it had been agreed,
That Harthacnut to the throne would succeed,
With Harold acting as England's trustee,
Whilst Harthacnut was across the sea.

With Harthacnut defending his father's gains,
Enduring battle and a dozen pains,
The church in England had prepared,
That Harold as king should be declared.

So Harthacnut in Denmark duly remained,
His rights and ambition there contained,
Whilst Harold's rule seemed undisputed,
While his brother felt he was better suited.

Yet the head of the church made him wait,
Two years until he felt the weight,
Of England's crown for which he longed,
While many believed his brother wronged.

Then, in the very same year of his coronation,
Some refused their loyal prostration.
Edward and Alfred, his stepbrothers contrived,
To see Harold deposed and of power deprived.

But his brother's actions were too daring,
There plans for Harold far too glaring,
And they were defeated with Alfred seized,
Leaving Harold supreme and well pleased.

Harold had moved too fast to be caught,
Moved too fast by brothers who sought,
To end his life, extinguish his flame,
But 'Harefoot' was also Harold's name.

No doubt Harold had many ideas,
To rule as king and remove any fears,
That he was able, the man for the task,
But death gave Harold a different mask.

After five years of rule, Harold was dead,
But few were in doubt of who'd rule instead.
So Harthacnut sailed to England to take,
The crown and his own England to make.

Harthacanut
(1040-1042)

Interesting fact:

His name in Danish means tough knot, and to the people he ruled he could be tough, especially when they were being taxed. He only ruled England for a couple of years, but had he lived longer, the Norman invasion might not have happened.

Already a king in his own right,
In Denmark where, in bloody fight,
He'd beaten the rebels who had tried,
To push his role of king aside.

He was the son of Cnut the Great,
Who'd forged an empire, a mighty state,
So Harthacnut would not permit,
A sleight to his pride to idly sit.

Harold, his brother, seized England's throne,
And Harthacnut was not alone,
In condemning the act, but he'd have to wait,
Until seeing his chance delivered by fate.

For Harold died after five long years,
With few, if any, shredding tears,
But it opened the way for Harthacnut,
To see his patience at last bear fruit.

He'd originally planned a different course,
Planning to land an invasion force,
But he'd been invited when he came,
Yet still took his army just the same.

Though when he saw that force wasn't needed,
Harthacnut finally conceded,
To raise a tax through different sources,
An unpopular tax to pay off his forces.

At last, in ten forty, he held in his hands,
Those rich and precious English lands,
Which had been conquered some time ago,
Yet his skills as a king were yet to show.

The lands in Norway would soon be lost,
Much to his and the empire's cost,
As he struggled to keep the empire as one,
But his rule in Norway seemed to be done.

Alfred's murder left his brother enraged,
So, a special show of power was staged,
Where Harold's body was dug up and defiled,
Treated like something bad and reviled.

Godwin, the earl of Wessex was accused,
Of the crime which saw the prince so abused,
But the king was able to show the court,
His innocence so the trial came to naught.

The king knew there'd be trouble in store,
Believing the earls were at the core,
Of all the mistrust which he had,
Suspicious of loyalty turning bad.

Used to ruling by his own decision,
And any advice just gained more suspicion,
The council of advisors was left in no doubt,
That with most decisions, they'd be left out.

Raising more taxes to increase the fleet,
At a time of bad harvest with less to eat,
People spoke out and many protested,
So, troops were sent while the King was detested.

Then an earl gave Harthacnut offence,
But the earl repented and had the sense,
To appeal to the king's mercy and grace,
But the king had already decided the case.

Harthacnut, the king, gave his word,
For safe conduct so the earl could be heard,
But in the earl's death he was a partaker,
And soon he was known as the great oath breaker.

He wouldn't have time to make things right,
To make amends to remove this blight,
For illness, which had dogged his existence,
Finally conspired to defeat his resistance.

Knowing that he was close to death's door,
Aware he'd lose that kingly chore,
Edward, his half-brother, was duly asked,
If, as new king, he'd be tasked.

Edward, was then duly invited,
And no doubt his mother was delighted,
To see her dynasty again extended,
A line where more could be descended.

The Saxons

Interesting fact:

The Saxons had been raiding Britain from across the sea long before the Romans left. In fact, it is believed that the Scottish word 'Sassenach' comes from the Gaelic word 'Sasunnach' meaning Saxon.

Edward The Confessor (1042-1066)

Interesting fact:

About a century after his death, the Pope made Edward a saint, and for almost two centuries he became one of England's main patron saints.

Son of Emma, and Ethelred the unready,
To some his reign was righteous and steady,
Focused on God and it being so long,
Edward believed that his path wasn't wrong.

With him the house of Wessex saw,
A return to rule like they'd seen before,
A rule that was long until it was taken,
By Cnut but hope was never forsaken.

Now the house of Wessex was back,
Its dynasty seemingly back on track,
Ready to rule all England once more,
Through shire, village, and shore to shore.

He'd spent some years with his mother abroad,
When Vikings conquered all by the sword,
Living across the sea in exile,
In Normandy which was not hostile.

Sweyn Forkbeard died in ten fourteen,
And with his death a return was seen,
Of Saxon rule, but not for too long,
As the Viking forces were too strong.

It was Ethelred who had been invited,
To return to England by nobles, excited,
Who wanted a Saxon king and prince,
To take the crown and the people convince.

Edward, though young, returned as well,
But once again the dynasty fell,
Meaning that Edward had to flee,
If he was to live and remain free.

So, Cnut ruled all England and that meant,
Edward had time to reflect and lament,
His family's beaten and wounded pride,
Living in exile where he'd have to abide.

Only when the last Viking king,
Had died would fate finally bring,
Edward's moment and his chance,
To come back home from Norman France.

Supported by Godwin, an Earl with power,
Edward knew this was his hour,
Where having faith had finally paid,
Faith that God would come to his aid.

In the city of Winchester, he was crowned,
With the nobles of England all around.
Edward knowing the earls were the key,
If he was to succeed with any degree.

Already powerful, Godwin received,
More power that many soon believed,
He was almost a king in his own right,
With perhaps the actual crown in his sight.

The king was aware his position was weak,
So, to make it better, Edward would seek,
A marriage to Godwin's daughter who,
Should make the Earl loyal and true.

Godwin's son was then also made,
An Earl as Edward was still afraid,
Of losing the loyalty of the great lords,
So bound them close with great rewards.

But Godwin's family members created,
More trouble than Edward had calculated,
With abduction and murder being used,
To gain more power with power abused.

Yet Edward was popular when he ended,
The tax for the ships which had defended,
England's shores from each possible raid,
The crews going home as they weren't paid.

And though the king was the wealthiest man,
For improving his lot, he had no plan,
With his lands being spread across the nation,
So, his base of power was in stagnation.

But in foreign affairs and religion too,
Edward was king and he also knew,
That he needed God to be on his side,
With God in all things being his guide.

Edward also liked to use those,
Whom he thought were wise and chose,
Many a Norman from lands where he'd been,
Living in exile with his mother, the Queen.

Yet Godwin was still the man who had,
More power than most which most thought bad.
So, when Edward rejected the Earl's candidate,
For the position of bishop, there followed hate.

When ordered to punish the gentry in Dover,
For causing some trouble, he let things boil over,
By siding with those who caused the mess,
Giving the king more worry and stress.

Godwin and Edward raised their forces,
With each determined to follow their courses.
Yet Godwin's men were far too unwilling,
To fight their king and do the Earl's killing.

Godwin had sought to win by the sword,
But had lost to the king, and then fled abroad.
He would return, and in no time at all,
He was restored to see enemies fall.

For a time, Edward managed to hold,
The spirit of Godwin, which had become bold,
But then Godwin died, leaving his son,
Harold to finish the plans that were spun.

The son's inheritance seemed to be weak,
The prospects for his house looking bleak,
But fate played its part to quickly restore,
The power and wealth he'd use and explore.

His brothers, too, were given position,
That only improved the family's condition,
Making their house second to none,
Yet taking the crown for now they'd shun.

Edward, by then, was more like a recluse,
Whilst Harold's family was let loose,
To rule in the king of England's stead,
With thoughts of Harold as king being bred.

The stress of ruling eventually stole,
Edward's strength but not his soul,
So, when he took his final breath,
His soul was God's upon his death.

Edward's marriage failed to achieve,
The heir he wanted his wife to conceive,
Which left the question of who'd succeed,
Of whether all parties would be agreed.

For Harold said he had a claim,
The Duke of Normandy thinking the same,
But only one would be able to win,
While each of their claims was rather thin.

Harold said that he was led,
By Edward's promise upon his deathbed,
Giving him England's coveted throne,
Which he'd be ruling sometime on his own.

Yet William's claim clearly stated,
That Edward's promise to him pre-dated,
That of Harold's, so William's was stronger,
Meaning that Harold could argue no longer.

As both had no proof, the argument stood,
Each one believing the other no good,
To wear England's crown, so came the need,
For both of the players to move with speed.

Harold moved first and was duly proclaimed,
King of England, leaving William inflamed.
William reacted by raising his forces.
Including the Norman knights and their horses.

The Duke of Normandy would sail prepared,
Though Harold planned he'd not land unimpaired,
So called the Saxons to prepare to defend,
Whatever the Norman Duke might send.

Later, this king would be given a name,
One which gave him considerable fame.
Trying hard not to be an evil transgressor,
Which is why he was called Edward the 'Confessor'.

Harold II (1066)

Interesting fact:

Harold was the last Anglo Saxon King to rule England, but the first monarch to be crowned in Westminster Abbey.

With Edward's death, Harold declared,
His plans for England would not be impaired,
So, he took the crown knowing too well,
He'd have to deal with whatever befell.

For the Duke of Normandy also aimed,
At taking the crown for which he was named.
Promised by words that by Edward were said,
That William would inherit when Edward was dead.

Harold was born to Godwin, who'd engaged,
In gaining more power, which so enraged,
The King and nobles who did their best,
To stop the earl, they'd fear and detest.

Harold's mother, Gytha, was a noble Dane,
Whose family, close to Cnut, would gain,
Much from their association,
Including much wealth and admiration.

Half Dane and half Saxon, he was viewed,
As Godwin's son, brave and shrewd.
But also best suited to represent,
The interests of all and was heaven sent.

For many years he had been schooled,
In politics, war and effectively ruled,
England whilst Edward to God would pray,
Leaving Harold to rule and have his say.

For Harold subdued all those who opposed,
All rival earls and lords who supposed,
That they could do better or just through hate,
Believed they could alter Harold's fate.

Though in Mercia Harold was forced to agree,
To Tostig, his brother, deposed as the fee,
For ending rebellion and to be true,
So Morcar, their leader, his threats withdrew.

Yet Harold wanted to secure the deal,
By taking a step he knew would seal,
Peace in the north and end all strife,
And took Morcar's sister for his wife.

At the beginning of January, ten sixty-six,
There started the desperate politics,
For England's crown with Edward's death,
But was Harold chosen by Edward's last breath?

Though William, the Norman, was no normal Duke,
And from the start he would rebuke,
Harold for not believing a word,
Of William's claim which should be heard.

William stated that Edward had sent,
Harold, the Earl, with word he'd consent,
To accepting William as rightful heir,
Something to which Edward would swear.

Harold's ship was wrecked off the coast,
Yet William was able to say and boast,
He rescued the earl who was now in his debt,
With more matters of honour being set.

For William stated that Harold asserted,
That he to William's claim was converted,
Promising all his support on the day,
When king Edward, by God, was taken away.

But soon that day had come and gone,
With only Harold's light which shone,
Leaving William's claim in the dark,
The truth of Harold's betrayal stark.

William felt he had little choice,
If he were to make Harold hear his voice,
So, he put together an audacious plan,
To defeat a king and beat Harold the man.

Harold knew that William would come,
They'd hear the sound of the beating drum,
As William and his army landed,
Hoping their courage would hold as demanded.

But as they waited, news soon came,
Of invasion which brought Harold much shame,
For Tostig, his brother, came to the north,
With the help of the Danes, he'd called forth.

The Viking king, Harald Hardrada,
Had visions of making a great Viking saga,
Encouraged by Tostig to sail and invade,
Telling him that's how the sagas were made.

Harold was forced to end his guard,
Of the southern coast and march very hard,
Towards the north to face his brother,
Where two brothers might face each other.

At Stamford Bridge, the armies met,
With a bloody encounter being set,
As Tostig was sure the foe was tired,
Harold's strength, by the march, almost expired.

Harold surprised them all by attacking,
The strength of his men never lacking,
And soon the invaders were being routed,
With Harold's victory never doubted.

News then arrived of William's invasion,
But his men didn't need too much persuasion,
To begin the long march back to the south,
With limbs that ached and a parched mouth.

In a few days, Harold's army approached,
The enemy which into England encroached,
With William and Harold well prepared,
To fight for a crown for which both of them cared.

Harold's army had the high ground,
With the Saxon shield wall looking sound,
Whilst William had to advance uphill,
Before he could close and begin the kill.

A couple of times, the Normans seemed,
Defeated and running as Harold had dreamed,
But this was due to a cruel mistake,
When word of William's death proved fake.

Yet still the Saxon shield wall held,
But many of Harold's troops were felled,
And finally, Harold received the blow,
That laid the king of England low.

William's men had succeeded in breaking,
The Saxon wall which had been taking,
The force of arrows, swords and knights,
And this defeat meant the end of their rights.

For Harold himself was amongst the slain,
So, with his death came William's gain,
Whose England he would shape and bend,
With Saxon rule at last at an end.

For just nine months, Harold was hailed,
As king of England and almost prevailed.
But though he was known as king in his court,
His dreams of rule were cut very short.

The Normans

Interesting fact:

Originally known as Norsemen, under their leader Rollo these Vikings had defeated the Franks and carved out a kingdom in Northern France.

William The Conqueror (1066-1087)

Interesting fact:

As a young boy, William was put into the care of a succession of guardians after his father died. However, successive guardians died as the nobles around him knew that whoever controlled William would have the rule and power of the duchy.

From a start in life that wasn't secure,
Where surviving childhood wasn't sure,
William found himself in possession,
Of England because of his aggression.

Throughout his life he'd always known,
Threat of death by plots that were sewn,
Growing up in a world of constant suspicion,
In fear of those with dangerous ambition.

Yet, despite the plots of his distant youth,
The Saxon world knew the awful truth,
Of how their King had been defeated,
The rule of Saxon England unseated.

William the Conqueror was aware,
He'd have to move with speed and care,
If his new title and new acquisition,
Was to improve his general condition.

For William knew there were still those,
Who'd want to exchange their threats and blows,
Always fighting against his power,
Making the struggle bitter and sour.

So, William did what he'd done in the past,
Taking firm action and moving fast,
Taking his army to London, and there,
He was crowned with pomp and flair.

But the sense of occasion and of awe,
Was ruined when his soldiers saw,
Some smoke which his men quickly perceived,
Was rebellion and they had been deceived.

Despite the innocent blood which was shed,
The crown was set upon William's head,
A sacred act witnessed by many,
With those opposing few if any.

The Norman King would then set in motion,
Rewards to his men who'd shown their devotion,
Giving lands and titles to each warring Knight,
Men who'd shed blood in many a fight.

Each noble he made would act as a warning,
To rebels who, for England, were mourning,
As the Normans built castles to keep control,
To govern, tax and keep peace as a whole.

In London he built a castle of stone,
In the city where his strength was shown,
The tower of London, the seat of his power,
To make the Saxon obey and to cower.

Yet Motte and Bailey were just the beginning,
As Normans were also concerned about sinning,
So, the king and his bishops began to search,
For places to build a cathedral and church.

But whilst William tried his best to frustrate,
All thoughts of rebellion and consolidate,
His position as king and ruler of all,
In the north some tried to see his reign fall.

Led by Hereward, the Saxons freely,
Raided the country based at Ely,
Where they were protected by a mighty fen,
A place to hide an army of men.

But these were just stubborn acts,
A matter of time before those tracks,
Across the fens were then betrayed,
With the subjugation merely delayed.

But the problems all these rebellion caused,
In revenue lost, yet the King never paused,
In giving orders to make the north pay,
To make all the rebels rue the day.

The soldiers destroyed as their king had bidden,
Destroying and killing unless it was hidden,
Harrying the north to demonstrate,
How rebels were always left desolate.

For decades, lands that were destroyed,
Those lands where peasants had been employed,
Were no longer fit for living or growing,
With the hunger on faces very soon showing.

In time, King William felt assured,
He was accepted as king and Lord,
Which meant, at last, he had the chance,
To return to matters back in France.

William's reign, at times, was marred,
By reactions and how he came down hard,
On those he thought threatened his peace,
For which his energies would never cease.

What's more, he had an eye for taxation,
Believing there shouldn't be relaxation,
In trying to get all the monies owed,
From noble to peasant and the field he sowed.

So, scribes across the land were dispatched,
That details for tax might be taken and matched,
To allow the king to demand each pay,
Their due as written in the Book of Doomsday.

It took less than a year to record everything,
And William could see that it would bring,
A great understanding of what was owed,
And the names of the people in each abode.

In less than a year, the book was completed,
Though not with joy by so many greeted,
As it gave the king the chance to collect,
The taxes he saw to be correct.

But William, who saw how things had been wrong,
Would not be able to enjoy things for long,
For in ten eighty-seven, while on campaign,
The King, while fighting, by chance was slain.

Some said an injury on his horse took him off,
While others believed a sickly cough,
But whatever it was, it left many confused,
As courtiers left, their minds bemused.

At Rouen, the king of England lay,
As nobles decided to slip away,
His body left to be robbed and stripped,
As each courtier off to his own land slipped.

The Normans did much to build and improve,
The old Saxon ways and also remove,
All which to William was seen as confronting,
Even peasants removed for the sake of his hunting.

William II (Rufus) (1087-1100)

Interesting fact:

Later writers speak of William as being quite a strong man, although they also write of how his stomach stuck out and his eyes were different colours to each other.

To William the Conqueror he was born,
Few had expected the crown to be worn,
By the third son they thought would remain,
A prince and never a throne attain.

When young, the boy would be given the name,
Of Rufus, which the boy could blame,
Upon the colour of his red hair,
Or perhaps his complexion, which wasn't fair.

Yet fate took a hand to change his path,
Leaving him king in its aftermath,
When an elder brother died in a hunt,
Putting William nearer the front.

What's more, his eldest brother had,
Been promised that his father would add,
Normandy to his other estates,
If he obeyed his father's dictates.

To Robert, the brother, this was a disaster,
That William should be England's master,
But there was little Robert could do,
Though resentment for his brother grew.

To add to the insult and make matters worse,
Robert the Duke would have to nurse,
Thoughts of his brother having dominion,
Over him as the king with a King's opinion.

But William would do his very best,
To honour his father's dying bequest,
By working hard to keep the peace,
With everyday issues which wouldn't cease.

In Scotland, he managed to assert,
His royal authority and so avert,
The need for campaign that was expensive,
Though England's wealth was extensive.

Even in Wales people had to confess,
How the King enjoyed such great success,
In bringing the Welsh under his control,
Through action and words used to cajole.

On the field of battle, William was brave,
Showing his foes how a king should behave,
A man who could set an example to all,
Who, in the saddle, sat proud and tall.

Yet, by his actions and each deed,
Some nobles felt angry and saw the need,
Of doing their best to show and prove,
Here was a king they had to remove.

When some nobles decided they had to strike,
To show their king bad faith and dislike,
William showed he was swift to engage,
Punished the nobles with brutal rage.

To all around it was plain and clear,
That William kept dissenters in fear.
Whilst also ruling with wisdom and reason,
His rage was harsh when dealing with treason.

But, in the end, William failed,
To leave an heir who would be hailed,
The next in his father's royal line,
Because taking a wife he would decline.

Whatever reason for not taking a bride,
And many reasons by foes were implied,
William did not have a queen to bare,
The sons to give his line an heir,

But his rule was seen in many eyes,
As that which was just, brave and wise,
Until, one day, whilst out hunting deer,
An arrow struck which proved too severe.

William's death was unexpected,
With suspicion being detected,
Yet nothing was ever really proved,
When the king of England was removed.

William, as king, was very able,
Though his temper could be quite unstable.
And once his reign had finally expired,
His brother Henry with the crown was attired.

Henry I
(1100-1135)

Interesting fact:

Henry used capable men to help run the country, allowing 'new men' to rise through the ranks based on their abilities. He was also the first King to establish the Royal Exchequer, which allowed successive governments to manage their finances.

When William the Conqueror had passed away,
His sons would squabble and try to play,
The game of who had the right to rule,
To show who was the best and who the fool.

Henry was the youngest and so,
William's will would clearly show,
His brothers would be given it all,
With Henry's portion being small.

His brother, Robert, inherited land,
In Normandy, where, he made a stand,
Against King William, who, he contended,
Should not be king and the will be amended.

In Normandy, Henry chose to reside,
With Robert where pressure was applied,
To help make the younger brother part,
With his wealth, but Henry was too smart.

For Henry wanted lands of his own,
His desire for greater status known,
So, Robert agreed to make him a count,
If he handed over the agreed amount.

Yet his elder brothers constantly fought,
As domination by each was sought,
Yet the younger brother had decided,
His strength with William would be sided.

Invasion plans by Robert were wasted,
The bitter taste of failure tasted,
With Robert's dreams not realised,
With the scrapping of plans he'd devised.

Over time, alliances adjusted,
As the brothers knew they couldn't be trusted,
With all of them jostling to defeat the other,
More like enemies than loving brother.

In time, it was William who had gained,
The edge over Robert, who was contained,
With Henry still weakest of the three,
Yet fate changed all by its decree.

Robert and William had signed a pact,
Where the Duke, by William, would be backed,
In helping Robert to fight and regain,
Any lands which were lost and titles maintain.

Yet through this agreement, it was revealed,
That Henry's fate and position was sealed,
As though his brother's pact was brittle,
As it still left Henry with very little.

Henry saw himself excluded,
From the crown by the pact they'd concluded,
So, Henry went to war with his kin,
With very little chance that he'd win.

Besieged in the fortress of Mont-Saint-Michelle,
The strength of his brother's forces would tell,
But Henry escaped, and started to roam,
Through northern France in search of a home.

And the pact his brothers had forged at Rouen,
Didn't last very long, and soon it was gone,
So, Henry's and William's forces united,
With Henry's hopes for the future excited.

In ten ninety-five, the fighting was stalled,
When a crusade by Pope Urban was called,
In which Duke Robert lost no time in enlisting,
Which his brothers were only too glad in assisting.

With troublesome Robert going on crusade,
A better relationship was soon made,
Between William and Henry, who then appeared,
Together often as the air seemed cleared.

Henry was there when the arrow shot,
Took William's life and ended his lot,
Leaving Henry to move and quickly seize,
The crown of England with relative ease.

Many promises to barons and earls were made,
In hopes that Henry could persuade,
The nobles of England to support,
Changes to policy which were sought.

King Henry knew he'd have to reward,
Supporters if he were to move toward,
The England which he hoped to achieve,
With supporters expecting to receive.

He also knew he'd have to take,
A bride as much would be at stake,
So having a queen might help produce,
An heir and future problems reduce.

Matilda of Scotland was selected,
Whose family line was respected,
For Saxon blood ran in her veins,
Helping the King with his recent gains.

They had two legitimate heirs,
Though more were born by Henry's affairs,
But a legitimate son was his to cherish,
With hopes his line would never perish.

But his brother Robert wasn't finished yet,
With the Duke's force looking set,
To try an invasion given the chance,
With the Duke adopting an aggressive stance.

Robert invaded and to him flocked,
Nobles whose plans by Henry were blocked.
Men of wealth with great ambition,
Who formed with Robert a coalition.

But yet again war was evaded,
As words and promises by them were traded,
Leaving Henry to deal with those now afraid,
Of the king's revenge for faith betrayed.

The peace with his brother wouldn't last,
As neither could ever forget the past,
With each viewing the other as a threat,
To be caught by the other in other's net.

The struggle for power would be taken,
To France where Robert's power was shaken,
By Henry's advance and constant attacks,
Meaning Duke Robert could never relax.

At last, with the duke finally held,
The constant struggle was finally quelled.
Henry could rule as he preferred,
His absolute rule no longer blurred.

Yet the king of France had demanded,
That Henry's allegiance to him be handed,
Henry responded by making alliance,
With foreign princes to avoid compliance.

Whilst also in Wales, nobles there,
Were unwilling to acknowledge or to swear,
Loyalty to Henry, so armies were sent,
To crush all rebellion and all dissent.

It seemed Henry's life was one big endeavour,
To deal with struggles that went on forever,
And more came his way on a sailing trip,
When his only son was lost with a ship.

Henry had fought all his problems and won,
But nothing prepared him for losing his son.
When news came, it was with disbelief,
Yet a king was felled by his sense of grief.

Despite the loss of the son to follow,
The wealth and power which to be hollow,
Henry had a nephew at court,
Stephen, who as a ruler was taught.

Troubles began when his brothers were handed,
Their father's power and he was left stranded,
With nothing but title, and some treasure,
Some said bad luck or his father's displeasure.

Stephen (1135-1154)

Interesting fact:

Stephen was very wealthy and well-liked by most people, rich and poor alike, and the cause of his wealth was mostly down to the clever workings of his wife, Matilda.

When Henry the First's son had drowned,
Concern arose about who'd be crowned,
But Stephen moved quickly to seize,
The crown to bring his foes to their knees.

Of noble birth, Stephen was raised,
At his uncle's court and was praised,
For bravery and his noble bearing,
Encouraged by his uncle's caring.

With the throne of England in his hands,
Along with his other Norman lands,
Stephen could see that he was well placed,
To deal with issues that had to be faced.

Trouble would come from Henry's daughter,
Which led to many years of slaughter,
As the daughter, Matilda, claimed to hold,
Promises which her father told.

Though Stephen refused and declined,
To believe her words and was inclined,
To deny her claim and so took it all,
To maintain law and order and let her fall.

But her husband, the Count of Anjou,
To his wife's just claim would remain true,
By attacking Stephen's lands in France,
By taking a more aggressive stance.

Geoffrey Plantagenet was the count,
Who, through Stephen's lands would mount,
Many attacks to make the point,
That he was the wrong one to anoint.

Then Matilda's half-brother also rebelled,
Which, to many, also spelled,
The end which many now could tell,
Was the sound of Stephen's death knell.

Before very long, Matilda invaded,
With lords in the south quickly persuaded,
To join her cause and then pursue,
King Stephen whose supporters were few.

At Lincoln, in battle, Stephen was caught,
Imprisoned and then many people thought,
Matilda had won and she'd assume,
The crown for herself and Stephen a tomb.

But Matilda's brother was captured too,
By Stephen's allies, so hope then grew,
That exchange of hostages might be made,
Though hostilities weren't about to fade.

This war went on with neither side slacking,
Each consumed with siege and attacking.
Stephen wanted his line to survive,
Through Eustace, his son, to which he'd strive.

Yet the Pope in Rome bluntly refused,
To grant the wish, leaving Stephen bemused,
So, the king was left to argue his case,
Arguing with clergy just to save face.

And all the while, the war went on,
With the voice of reason seemingly gone,
As Matilda and Stephen, their forces arrayed,
Their parts in the power struggle were played.

When Matilda's troops in England landed,
By her son Henry being commanded,
Stephen was faced by a strong collection,
Of enemies heading in his direction.

For many nobles had made the decision,
To add to the chaos and division,
By joining Matilda's legitimate cause,
Much to many people's applause.

With such a great force to try and defeat,
Or even if he was forced to retreat,
Stephen knew the war would persist,
While hate and mistrust was allowed to exist.

Yet nobles on each side were unwilling,
To carry on with the constant killing.
Stephen and Matilda were forced to accept,
An end to the anarchy which had to be kept.

What helped Stephen to make this accord,
Was the death of the son whom he adored,
Leaving the kingdom without a successor,
Apart from the woman who was the aggressor.

Talks were held, and it was agreed,
That Matilda's son, Henry, would succeed,
With Stephen's other son being omitted,
Passed over so England benefitted.

Stephen would rule and not be deprived,
As long as his health and wellbeing thrived,
But when he died, the agreement asserted,
That all to Matilda's line reverted.

Just a year later, in eleven fifty-four,
England and Normandy finally saw,
The start of the reign of the house of Anjou,
Whose power, for a while, only grew.

Stephen's reign, like those before,
Was dogged by unrest, intrigue and war,
Though peace, by all, was gladly received,
Even though by such ways achieved.

The House of Plantagenet (The Angevins)

Interesting fact:

The house of Plantagenet originally came from the Duchy of Anjou, a large area in the centre of France that was always struggling with the surrounding duchies for power, wealth and influence over each other.

Henry II
(1154-1189)

Interesting fact:

When he was just seventeen years old, Henry was made Duke of Normandy, gaining the same title as his predecessor, William the Conqueror, before he invaded England.

His reign was born from bloody feud,
Planned when peace by all was sued.
This would leave Matilda's son,
The king when Stephen's reign was done.

Already versed in the bloody art,
Of war and plots from the start,
Henry would show his true ambition,
As he brought his opponents to submission.

When just a young man, he was wed,
To Eleanor, who'd left a marriage bed,
When marriage to the king of France had ended,
Which meant Henry's lands were then extended.

For his wife was Eleanor of Aquitaine,
Whose lands and wealth Henry would gain,
And together they would help to raise,
Eight children, much to the people's praise.

Restoring those royal lands in Touraine,
Regaining lands in Anjou and Maine,
He saw his power and wealth increase,
Once his true plans saw release.

For Henry was full of determination,
After much thought and deliberation,
To regain lost titles and therefore expand,
His power, wealth and scope of his land.

Yet his ambition would quickly lead,
To tension with France, which loathed to concede,
Lands the French king duly believed,
Were his, which left England and France aggrieved.

Louis the Seventh of France resisted,
Henry's aggression and still insisted,
That Henry had no right to take,
Louis' lands or his claims to make.

Treaties were held and words were spoken,
But always the peace was quickly broken,
When both of the Kings saw their chance,
To regain or seize their piece of France.

For decades this quarrel went to and fro,
With neither prepared to let something go,
Yet Henry's advantage was quite clear,
Gaining more lands to extend his frontier.

Yet while he showed he was ruthless abroad,
Which Henry's supporters would applaud,
He'd find more trouble closer to home,
Whilst trying to reform the church of Rome.

For Henry wanted to improve and reform,
Relationships which were very lukewarm.
Then the Archbishop of Canterbury ruled,
That in matters of faith he'd not be schooled.

Thomas Becket, had excommunicated,
Bishops who hadn't appreciated,
His authority as the head of the church,
Believing they sought to usurp and besmirch.

In a pique of anger, Henry declared,
He wished his royal person was spared,
From Bishops and clerics who only gave,
Troubles to hound him to the grave.

Hearing his comment, some knights agreed,
That Henry, from all the woe, should be freed,
So, they went to Canterbury to defend,
Their master's rights and a bishop's life end.

But, once Henry heard of Thomas's death,
He fell with grief and was short of breath,
As he knew Thomas's death was very wrong,
Just one passing comment all along.

Though Henry and Thomas had disagreed,
On religious matters, the King saw a need,
To repent for the words he'd uttered in haste,
Knowing that many viewed him with distaste.

But those who left the bishop dead,
Had quit the scene and already fled.
Having sinned, the pope in Rome declared,
Time as Crusaders would see their souls spared.

Not only did Henry have to contend,
With religious turmoil but he had to defend,
From his sons who seemed to want only more,
Which meant more turmoil was in store.

As the Angevin empire had expanded,
Henry's five sons had each demanded,
A bigger piece of the empire to own,
As each had watched as the empire had grown.

Whatever was given, was not enough,
With the sons believing their treatment was rough,
So, rebellion followed and was assisted,
By the king of France whose help was enlisted.

The Great Revolt was only subdued,
By Henry's commanders, able and shrewd.
But peace didn't last, and once again,
Sons of the king threatened his reign.

By eleven eighty-nine, two sons had died,
Killed by rebellion they had tried,
And Henry himself was fading fast,
But his legacy would for many years last.

For Henry's reforms in law would create,
The basis for the future state,
Out of which the people could draw,
Security within the common law.

King Philip of France and Prince Richard had,

Defeated Henry whose condition was bad.

His father near death, Richard shed few tears,

As the death would end everyone's fears.

Richard I
(The Lion heart)
(1189-1199)

Interesting fact:

Despite being born in England, when he was made King, Richard spent as little as six months in the country. Known for his bravery, he commanded his first army when he was just sixteen years old.

Many a tale would be told,
Of how King Richard, young and bold,
Fought his enemies whilst still young,
Recounting deeds in songs that were sung.

Not very old when battle was seen,
Richard showed that he was so keen,
To prove to man and God that he,
Would not from battle turn and flee.

His elder brothers were expected to rule,
But fate would deal a hand so cruel,
Taking his brothers, one by one,
So, Richard was left as the ruling son.

Richard had trained from an early age,
In how to fight and war to wage,
Taking part in the joust and melee,
With cheering and the horse's neigh.

Few in the realm were quite so brave,
As the King who always fought and gave,
All his energy to war and glory,
Always enhancing his personal story.

Tall, handsome, trained and skilled,
Without concern for enemies killed,
Here was a king who was greatly admired,
Whose skill in war others duly aspired.

Yet war in itself was not sufficient,
Though Richard was always very proficient,
In winning and showing a chivalric side,
But often his anger would not hide .

It was just as well that Richard knew,
The art of war as troubles grew,
With rebellions in his father's lands,
With troubles caused by foreign hands.

Yet his lands in France had always been,
A source of trouble where war was seen,
As the Kings of France were committed,
To having their claims on the lands admitted.

But Richard, the warrior, was always prepared,
To face any threats his enemies dared,
Charging forth to defend his rights,
Ready to face any king and his knights.

It was whilst young Richard was on campaign,
Fighting for father in Aquitaine,
That Richard's prowess set him apart,
Gaining the name of 'Lionheart'.

All the while, Richard would play,
A political game to see the day,
When he might be at last rewarded,
With title of King and all homage afforded.

For his dealings with his father were tense,
The pressure between the two immense,
With the father not trusting him at all,
While the son plotted to see his fall.

At last, Richard would manage to gain,
The King of France's help to maintain,
His rightful claim to his father's throne,
As his was the right and his alone.

Then, as king, came a cause of attraction,
A noble quest that would be a distraction,
When news arrived of a Christian defeat,
Where the enemy's victory was complete.

The Holy Land was about to be lost,
A land that was taken at a terrible cost,
With Jerusalem itself being taken back,
By Muslim skill and their attack.

So, Richard took the oath of the cross,
To fight to redeem the Christian loss,
Taking an army to land in the east,
That the sacred land might be released.

Having done all he could to raise the coin,
Richard left England with hopes to join,
The others who'd vowed to join the quest,
Who saw themselves as Christendom's best.

King Philip of France had also agreed,
To join the crusade with God's speed,
So that both of the Kings wouldn't fear,
The taking of lands as they were both near.

They sailed from ports where people waved,
Confident God would see them saved,
From risks the journey had to bring,
Buoyed up by psalms that all would sing.

Sailing across the sea was a risk,
Compared to walking, the journey was brisk,
Taking the fleet to Sicily,
Where he landed horse and infantry.

But there king Richard became involved,
In the politics which on the island evolved,
Whilst people in Messina rebelled,
With hopes the Crusaders might be expelled.

Richard reacted with brutal force,
The sack of Messina taking its course,
Showing the people war's grim face,
With Richard then using the town as his base.

But tensions grew amongst the allies,
Which threatened all their Crusader ties.
In April, Richard set sail for Acre,
Chancing his luck on surf and breaker.

His luck never held, and his fleet separated,
Yet soon discovered where most were located,
Finding themselves on Cyprus stranded,
Where, by chance, they had landed.

Richard's betrothed was also there,
Berengaria who'd come to share,
Some of the perils her fiancée might face,
Though she was almost lost without trace.

Richard learnt that she was held,
By the ruler of Cyprus, whose arrogance swelled,
By refusing to let Berengaria go,
So, Richard attacked and laid Cyprus low.

Many leaders from the Holy Land came,
Drawn by Richard's growing fame,
As a king whose skills as a fighter were growing,
His deeds of chivalry constantly showing.

With the important island of Cyprus taken,
His faith in the cause no longer shaken,
Richard proceeded to Acre at last,
His power and his reputation vast.

Though before he departed, Richard led,
His betrothed to the altar and they were wed,
Making Berengaria England's Queen,
Yet she by the English would never be seen.

In June of eleven ninety-one,
The course and promise having been run,
Richard and his army at last came ashore,
To face the enemy and even the score.

In the siege of Acre, Richard fell ill,
And unable to walk Richard was still,
Able to lead and direct the assault,
To the place the defence was at fault.

At last, the city was forced to surrender,
By promises made to each defender.
Very soon King Richard was holding,
Thousands of prisoners as plans were unfolding.

The Muslim leader, Saladin, knew,
Crusaders would always have to remain true,
To move on Jerusalem if they dared,
But staying in Acre could mean being ensnared.

Richard also knew the threat,
Of staying in Acre, getting caught in the net,
So decided to move along the coast,
To avoid Saladin and the Muslim host.

Yet before he left, orders were given,
That his three thousand prisoners should be driven,
At the point of the sword to be executed,
With noble chivalry sorely polluted.

Richard believed he could only move on,
If the worry of having prisoners was gone,
And once the burden had been removed,
Richard believed the odds had improved.

Moving south, he was soon presented,
With Saladin's forces who deeply resented,
The way the Crusaders had badly treated,
Prisoners from Acre who'd been defeated.

But at Arsuf, Saladin's forces were beaten,
Their words of outrage had to be eaten,
Leaving Richard to head for the prize,
Seeming invincible in everyone's eyes.

By late November, having come so far,
Nothing, it seemed, could victory bar,
When Richard's army came within sight,
Of Jerusalem's walls and the final fight.

But it was already late in the year,
And Richard had a nagging fear,
That a siege before the city wall,
Might see him trapped before the fall.

Richard did not want to risk a defeat,
So ordered his army to slowly retreat,
Asking his army to give up its goal,
The object so dear to everyone's soul.

Winter would pass, and when summer came,
Both sides renewed their bitter game,
Of Crusaders advancing to just within sight,
Of Jerusalem's walls, but not giving fight.

Fighting and then negotiations failed,
With plans from both the leaders derailed,
And Richard knew that wherever he'd roam,
His brother John plotted at home.

At last, King Richard could wait no more,
So negotiated an end to the war.
Forced to quit his mighty crusade,
Aware his brother's plans were laid.

Yet the shadow of bad fortune would cast,
Its darkness over the King and last,
Until his feet trod on English soil,
When all his enemies plans he'd foil.

The journey home saw Richard arrested,
By enemies who were deeply invested,
In making Richard pay for those times,
When his acts were seen, by some, as crimes.

For two long years, he was confined,
As a captive until his nobles could find,
The money to pay for the ransom asked,
With the whole of England being tasked.

Much was sacrificed and sold,
To raise sufficient ransom gold,
But the king of England was set free,
Which most of the people were happy to see.

Whilst in prison, Richard's brother, John,
Had rebelled and much depended on,
King Philip of France, who made some gain,
Hoping Richard was held or even slain.

Forgiving John, Richard proceeded,
To reclaim that which could not be conceded,
And war with Philip would only persist,
While each, to the other, would try to resist.

At Gisor, Richard would add more fame,
To what many thought was an apt noble name,
Adding more glory to his noble fight,
By using the motto: 'God and my Right'

Then in March of eleven ninety-nine,
Besieging a castle, and in front of the line,
He rode too close to the men in revolt,
And Richard was struck by a crossbow bolt.

The bolt itself hadn't struck to kill,
But the wound festered, and so would kill,
The lionhearted king who thought,
Nobility lay in the way a king fought.

John
(1199-1216)

Interesting fact:

When he was young, John was nicknamed 'Lackland' because being the youngest of four sons he wasn't expected to inherit anything, let alone a whole kingdom.

The brother of Richard, the absent King,
The reign of John was set to bring,
More trouble to a troubled land,
As nobles and King each made a stand.

Yet John was favoured by London's mob,
Who planned with John to scheme and rob,
Richard's man he'd nominated,
While John's new order dominated.

John had promised the people much,
By noble words which seemed to touch,
The hearts of London's City folk,
By saying he'd free them from their yolk.

With London and its people bought,
The throne of England could be sought,
Then John to Richard's captors said,
Hold the king, don't release instead.

Yet Richard's and John's mother acted,
By raising the ransom whilst John was distracted,
Which saw King Richard come home at last,
While John begged his brother for forgiveness, fast.

But Richard knew John must be the heir,
The rightful person to leave the care,
Of ruling England when Richard was dead,
A noble Prince to rule in his stead.

It wasn't too long before John had his chance,
When Richard died whilst warring in France,
But John wasn't saddened by his loss,
The death didn't tarnish victory's gloss.

Then Arthur, John's nephew, tried to make,
A bid for the throne and hoped to take,
Those lands in France England held,
The loss of which disaster spelled.

In twelve 0-three, John had created,
The start of the Royal Navy, located,
At Portsmouth at the newly built base,
With ships improved for the trials they'd face.

But John's reputation was dealt a blow,
By tales of murder which people would sow,
Of a niece kidnapped and Arthur killed,
Or so the stories of intrigue spilled.

The war with his nephew had left England weak,
Which gave the French king a chance to seek,
The reclaiming of lands lost long ago,
To which end King Phillip wasn't slow.

John lost money and power too,
Which meant there was only one thing to do,
So, he introduced several acts,
One of which was the first income tax.

Then came disputes with church and pope,
When John began to plan and hope,
After Archbishop of Canterbury, Hubert, died,
John's bid for the post with his own man was tried.

The Chapter of Bishops soon objected,
With John's appointed man rejected,
And soon the Pope himself was involved,
With disputes and arguments not soon resolved.

John seized incomes which belonged to the church,
While the Pope in Rome began to search,
For ways to punish the wayward John,
Angry and sad for the path he was on.

At last, King John was forced to concede,
To the pope's authority and the need,
To try to obey the pope's decrees,
To forget the idea of 'do as he please'.

But the war with France kept up apace,
With John losing land and losing face,
With the Battle of Bouvines in twelve fourteen,
Being the ultimate, humiliating scene.

Being forced to agree to a humbling peace,
The war with France would finally cease,
But John's prestige as king was now flawed,
With nobles and commons no longer awed.

With the war lost and taxation high,
Up went a loud rebellious cry,
And forty barons made their move,
Marching on London, their point to prove.

In twelve fifteen, John was compelled,
To sign Magna Carta, with the changes it held,
But John soon appealed to the pope for support,
Claiming he'd signed it because he was caught.

The pope agreed that John could betray,
The charter he'd signed and go his own way,
Ruling as king and not as a subject,
Regaining his power and his respect.

War with the barons would quickly follow,
With all of John's plans and boasts proving hollow,
As France once more became involved,
Assisting the barons that the war be resolved.

Outnumbered and forced to retreat from his foes,
Instead of surrender or terms John chose,
To move from place to place until,
At Newark Castle he fell desperately ill.

Suffering from dysentery, and growing weak,
Unable to travel and barely to speak,
On eighteenth October, twelve sixteen,
So ended a life that was less than serene.

Henry III
(1216 – 1272)

Interesting fact:

Henry was a very religious man and would often be seen in tears during a sermon in church. As such, he gave large sums of money to various charities, but persecuted the Jews, making them pay large sums of money to him.

Just a young boy when he ascended,
Succeeding his father, John, he defended,
Against the barons who had rebelled,
Until the rebellion had been quelled.

Though only young, Henry declared,
Mercy was there, so many were spared,
With Henry even stating to all,
Magna Carta would stand, not fall.

Then he tried to regain what was lost,
In France so with his army he crossed,
The channel with dreams of reclaiming all,
But the plan failed, and dreams would fall.

Then, at home, there was an uprising,
Which, to Henry, was surprising,
Because he thought he'd won the respect,
Of all the nobles with none to suspect.

The church authorities saw the need,
To come to his aid and intercede,
Between the two warring factions,
With peace duly gained by their actions.

Henry then felt he'd have to rule,
By himself or fear being played the fool,
So, he relied on his wits and skill,
Choosing no senior position to fill.

By twelve thirty-six, Henry was wed,
To Eleanor of Provence of whom many had said,
Would give him the sons and serve him well,
Which would any fears of succession dispel.

With this formidable noble French bride,
Supporting his rule and by his side,
Henry was able to rule as required,
Active, pious to make laws as desired.

Not travelling as much as those Kings before,
Henry invested the money more and more,
On castles and palaces, he admired,
Buildings he liked which attention required.

Yet, though he was seen as a pious man,
Within the King some hatred ran,
Which he aimed at England's Jews,
Extracting large sums beyond their dues.

Those French lands which were lost and taken,
He tried to retrieve, but all was forsaken,
When his plans failed in a bloody fight,
Convincing the king diplomacy's might.

He then had the dream of going on a crusade,
To the Levant, so plans were laid,
But, in Gascony, sedition was sewn,
His dreams of glory he'd have to postpone.

Henry's style of rule had become a weight,
Which most of the people learned to hate,
As taxation and failed foreign polices showed,
God's blessing had not through Henry flowed.

The barons rebelled yet again,
Their objectives simple and plain,
To reform the government so England would,
Be ruled as they knew England could.

But this league of barons did not hold,
Their lack of unity quickly told,
So, Henry was able to rapidly seize,
The reins, but England was on its knees.

A stable government could not be achieved,
Which left the people uncertain, aggrieved,
But in twelve sixty-three a man took control,
Simon de Montfort who knew his role.

By seizing power, a new war erupted,
Barons and King thinking the other corrupted.
At the Battle of Lewes, Henry was taken,
But his son set him free, so all wasn't forsaken.

The barons had lost, and Henry sought,
To inflict harsh terms, but wise council was sought,
From the church which said mercy first,
So, Henry couldn't slake his vengeful thirst.

Rebuilding of trust and power took time,
And Henry, no longer, was in his prime,
But to win people over, he then persecuted,
The Jews, as hatred for them was deeply rooted.

Yet, for all his actions to regain prestige,
Time and cares took their toll with ease,
And his fifty-six years of king would end,
In twelve seventy-two, to some a godsend.

Edward I
(1272-1307)

Interesting fact:

Although he has been condemned for expelling the Jews from England, one of the good things Edward did was to set up the first Parliament by which he, and successive rulers, have been able to govern effectively.

Before he was king, Edward had,
Learned to rule whilst still a lad,
In Gascony as his father required,
Though Edward to greater powers aspired.

As part of the deal, Edward had wed,
Eleanor of Castile, and together they led,
A loving marriage which would last,
Forty-six years until Eleanor passed.

He was in the Baron's Wars involved,
But when this conflict was resolved,
He took the oath to go on crusade,
Where pious reputations often were made.

He was on his way back when he heard,
That his father, King Henry the Third,
Had finally died after so many years,
Though few, if any would shed many tears.

It wasn't until twelve seventy-four,
That Edward set foot upon England's shore,
Then crowned as Henry's rightful successor,
The crown, and England's, rightful possessor.

As king, Edward would try to reform,
The common law and not conform,
To what his nobles expected to see,
Showed he was from his father's traits free.

But his skill and attention were often drawn,
To war when rebellion at home was born,
Especially in Wales when the nobles decided,
A king of their own could be provided.

Twice they rebelled, and twice Edward went,
To crush the rebellions and troops were sent,
To make the Welsh sorely regret,
Their challenge to Edward, whose mind was set.

By twelve eighty-three, Wales was taken,
Rebellion to Edward shown as mistaken,
If they believed that the king would admit,
To releasing Wales and his plans to quit.

Then, as a symbol to show his intent,
Great sums of money would duly be spent,
Building castles and towns to keep Wales in line,
Acting as a strong royal sign.

Into these places, English people were placed,
Much to local people's distaste,
Then took from Wales its greatest treasure,
The Prince of Wales title for good measure.

Not long after Wales seemed subdued,
In the north more trouble brewed,
When a dispute about Scotland's succession,
Was taken to Edward for his intercession.

But Edward believed he could claim,
Feudal rights and therefore aim,
At making Scotland his very own,
With any chance of peace duly blown.

In the war that followed, the Scottish found,
How Edward's forces marched and ground,
Into the earth everyone who chose,
To stand and fight and exchange blows.

'The Hammer of the Scots' fought hard,
To defeat the Scots, but success was barred,
When Scotland's ally, France, stepped in,
Joining the war to deny him the win.

As the war dragged on, so expenses rose,
And Edward would not see its close,
Because in thirteen 0-seven, his time was done,
His path to make an empire run.

Edward had achieved so very much,
Applied his very determined touch,
To make his nation powerful, feared,
But, in the end, bankruptcy neared.

Though parliament was made more permanent,
No longer a powerless ornament,
His expulsion of all the Jews is seen,
As brutal, unfair and terribly mean.

When his wife, Eleanor, was taken away,
Edward's life seemed to go astray,
For though he remarried a younger bride,
He no longer had that love by his side.

Edward was seen as a king who was tough,
Tall, uncompromising and with enemies rough,
With the title 'Longshanks' duly applied,
Because of his height and taken with pride.

Edward II (1307-1327)

Interesting fact:

Edward was born in Wales and many prophets of the time declared that the new baby would be the new King Arthur, leading England to greatness and glory.

Three older brothers, meant that he,
Should not have dared to hope and see,
The day when England's crown was gained,
As older brothers should have reigned.

But brothers died and he was left,
Though few would say he was bereft,
As the crown was his, along with the power,
The wealth and strength to make foes cower.

A princess of France would be selected,
That relations with France might be protected,
So, the Princess Isabella came,
To marry the king as part of the game.

Yet Piers Gaveston was the King's pet,
His trusted friend and courtier yet,
The queen and barons envied his place,
So, Piers was killed to settle the case.

The barons had murdered Edward's friend,
And the king was not about to pretend,
To agree or like what the barons had done,
As intrigue and plots were carefully spun.

Years of conflict, spilling of blood,
Swept the land like terrible flood,
As barons and King sought to be,
Ruler, master and from the other one free.

Then, in Scotland, bad news arrived,
Because Robert the Bruce had contrived,
To push the English out of their land,
And at Bannockburn they made their stand.

Edward's army was truly defeated,
What was left had then retreated,
Carrying with it England's ambition,
Ruining further Edward's position.

With barons at home and Scots in the north,
Troubles were rife, but then came forth,
A mighty famine to add to the pain,
With the common people feeling the strain.

The people of England knew who to blame,
Knew from where all the troubles came,
So many spoke out about Edward's rule,
Of how their King was foolish and cruel.

They also complained of the family, who,
Advised the king and whose influence grew,
The Despensers who the barons despised,
For all the things they freely advised.

In a series of struggles, the barons failed,
To have their way, so the king was hailed,
As being triumphant, but not for long,
His sense of triumph turning out to be wrong.

Peace with Scotland he was forced to concede,

Then his wife, at last, saw the need,

Of helping to force her husband out,

As she listened to the popular shout.

Isabella had met one of Edward's Lords,

Who fled Edward's reach after they crossed swords,

But, together in France, they raised a small force,

Whose success, or defeat, would shape England's course.

Roger Mortimer was this man's name,

Whose nobility and intrigue were to gain fame,

For, together with the Queen, he ensured,

England's wish for change was secured.

Though Edward tried, he could not succeed,

In defeating his foes and was forced to heed,

The advice of those who still remained,

Whose trust and loyalty he still retained.

In thirteen twenty-seven, he abdicated,
His plans and dreams bitterly frustrated,
Stepping aside for his teenage son,
His time as ruler and King being done.

For those now in charge it was very clear,
The former king couldn't last the year,
And in Berkeley Castle, one September day,
The former King's life was taken away.

Edward III
(1327-1377)

Interesting fact:

Many people believed that the French intended to extinguish the English language, especially if they invaded or if England's ruling classes continued to prefer to use French. So, Edward decided that English would be used in law, and Parliament would always be opened using English too.

Edward was crowned at just fourteen,
Yet real power would not be seen,
As Roger Mortimer ruled instead,
With Edward's mother sharing Roger's bed.

After three years of being subjected,
To Roger's rule and feeling neglected,
Edward seized the power at last,
Leaving his days of fear in the past.

The king began with a fresh campaign,
In Scotland, with hopes to remove the stain,
From England's battered reputation,
By claiming much for his nation.

With Scotland defeated, he'd declare,
He was France's rightful heir,
Which the French duly declared,
Was wrong and for war prepared.

This dispute would set in motion,
A war of length and such emotion,
A hundred years, or so, of strife,
Where death and pain were always rife.

Success at Crecy and Poitiers too,
Meant that Edward's standing grew,
With territories by France surrendered,
With respect, by France, duly tendered.

Yet war abroad meant hard taxation,
From which there was no relaxation,
Leading to many feeling discontented,
Which they believed could be prevented.

But worse was to come when from the east,
A plague, which struck the best and the least,
Swept through the land killing many,
And, in some places, not sparing any.

It struck in thirteen forty-eight,

With no fortress, wall or city gate,

Offering any sort of defence,

So, the death and suffering were immense.

A third or more of the population,

Suffered pain and degradation,

When the disease took its hold,

Whether pauper, rich, young or old.

Yet the loss of souls helped to make,

A shortage of workers for nobles to take,

To work their fields, so workers said,

The old rate of pay, like the others, was dead.

Through legislation, Edward tried,

To deny the workers and stem the tide,

Of change that came due to the plague,

Though what would change still seemed vague.

But, in time, the plague diminished,
Though deaths and suffering hadn't finished,
Though Edward still sent troops to fight,
Upon French soil to show his might.

It was Edward, king Edwards eldest son,
Who, at the Battle of Poitiers, won,
A major victory and besides those who fell,
Took the French king and his son as well.

The Prince of Wales, known as the Black Prince,
Through his actions, would convince,
England and France of his uniqueness,
Who showed his skills and noble prowess.

Here was a son who seemed to be set,
To follow his father as king, and yet,
Disease was near and made him pay,
As dysentery took his life away.

The war in France was still inconclusive,
Victory, to Edward, was always elusive,
Which meant the taxes were incurred,
With dissenting voices heard.

Even the defeat and the taking,
Of France's King was not the breaking,
Of a bloody war that simply continued,
With occasional pauses, but always renewed.

For Edward, war had more appeal,
Than affairs of state, and the common weal,
Leaving much of England's administration,
With those he trusted, of good education.

Yet, those who were good, eventually died,
And from the effects he could not hide,
Which was a new and younger court,
Those who for the princes fought.

War with France started once more,
When a new French king clearly saw,
That the English hold needed to be,
Pushed from France to be set free.

With hostilities came the old demand,
For more taxation and good command,
Of the forces that needed to go and face,
The enemy and not suffer disgrace.

Edward sent John of Gaunt,
Another son who would flaunt,
England's pride and her reliance,
On an English prince to show her defiance.

Though French forces were assailed,
The plans of Edward's son had failed,
So, Edward had to at last resort,
To treaty and further plans to abort.

Failure in war, and financial stress,
Meant parliament could soon impress,
Upon more nobles to object to it all,
That which they saw might be England's fall.

The king was ill, so left his son John,
To deal with all that was going on,
But the prince was forced to then accept,
Parliament's demands that peace be kept.

By this time, Edward was dying,
Weak and ill and in his bed lying.
In thirteen seventy-seven, he never awoke,
After having had a massive stroke.

Richard II
(1377-1399)

Interesting fact:

He was married to his first wife, Anne, for twelve years but she died of plague. A couple of years later, Richard was betrothed to Isabella, the daughter of the French King, but she was just six years old at the time.

The Prince of Wales had died before,
His father, so, according to law,
King Edward's grandson would possess,
That mantle full of woe and stress.

Richard the Second was only ten,
A noble Prince of England, when,
He was crowned as rightful heir,
Exposed to every kingly care.

Yet he would not rule alone,
Though he was the one upon the throne,
As troubles from the past would haunt,
He and his uncle John of Gaunt.

A council was formed which was led,
By his uncle and nobles who were bred,
To live and advise as nobles should,
To serve the king as nobles would.

Being so young, Richard relied,

On what they said and to be his guide,

With much to do to help restore,

The economy because of disease and war.

But then in thirteen eighty-one,

A revolt of the peasants had begun,

Small at first, then increasingly growing,

With more discontent from the people showing.

Heading for London, approaching the city,

Led by Wat Tyler and a committee,

The peasants were angry about conditions,

Of taxes, and threats to their new positions.

For the plague had allowed so many to see,

How the man in the field at last could be free,

From bondage and from being tied,

To one single master on which he relied.

When a poll tax collector tried to collect,
Monies owed he was shown disrespect,
With protests growing from village to town,
With local authority simply cast down.

London was reached and almost sacked,
Royal officials stopped and attacked,
With the King himself fearing the worst,
When the army of peasants through the streets burst.

So, Richard agreed to a meeting to speak,
With Tyler in order not to look weak,
But during the meeting Tyler was struck,
Was killed and the rebels came unstuck.

For, shortly after, they all dispersed,
Their hopes and dreams soon all reversed,
As Richard's actions were quick and driven,
With the rebel leaders not forgiven.

Yet the Peasant's Revolt had been a scare,
And future policy would not dare,
To raise more taxes for war abroad,
As the acts of the peasants had left the King awed.

Besides, the king much rather preferred,
To listen to music or the spoken word,
To sounds of war and the trumpet blast,
Or more treasure into the furnace cast.

The King would try to cultivate,
An atmosphere of art not hate,
Where art and culture ruled the head,
Not war or plans to avenge England's dead.

Relying so much on a favoured few,
To lead and guide as he thought they knew,
Meant other nobles weren't included,
Which gave much strength to those excluded.

The Lords Appellant would take control,
Temporarily masters of the whole,
Until King Richard once more proved,
What Kings must do or else be removed.

He bided his time, but Richard would act,
Against those Lords who'd made a pact,
With many facing their execution,
As part of Richard's retribution.

For the next two years, Richard's rule,
To many seemed too harsh and cruel,
Which gave power to the discontent,
Though few would ever their feelings vent.

Then, when John of Gaunt had died,
His noble son, Henry Bolingbroke, vied,
With other nobles to try and replace,
Richard with someone they might all embrace.

Henry invaded with a small force,
But as it proceeded upon its course,
More and more people flocked to unite,
With the cause they considered to be right.

In June of thirteen ninety-nine,
Richard's few followers saw the sign,
Of a man whose cause was now lost,
Where the line of defeat had now been crossed.

With little effort, the king was deposed,
With a replacement being proposed,
And while the new man looked to many so well,
Richard would die in his dungeon cell.

The House of Lancaster

Interesting fact:

The house was created when Henry III established the Earldom of Lancaster for his second son, Edmund 'Crouchback'.

Henry IV
(1399-1413)

Interesting fact:

Henry was the first monarch in over three hundred years whose first language was English and not Norman French.

He was the grandson of Edward the Third,
So, within his royal blood there stirred,
Those feelings of royalty that he knew,
Belonged to just a noble few.

When John of Gaunt, his father, died,
His inheritance by the king denied,
Henry was helped to take the throne,
Left Richard to die in a cell alone.

Bolingbroke Castle is where he was born,
The epithet stayed and so was worn,
As a symbol of noble power and pride,
Which, like his lineage, he'd never hide.

But the former king Richard had made the mistake,
Of thinking this nobleman would forsake,
His rights as a Duke and simply accept,
Richard's act and the lands which he'd kept.

When Henry moved, all England saw,
That he, by most nobles, was favoured more,
Which meant that he had enough support,
To face the King wherever he sought.

With Richard's defeat, and his son ignored,
This claim to the throne was one to applaud,
As it ended the rule of a King much despised,
Leaving Richard alone and chastised.

One of Henry's first moves was to declare,
The Duchy of Lancaster would be there,
As a title which monarchs of England would,
Hold forever as only they could.

A somewhat pious and religious man,
Henry helped the church by devising a plan,
Which sought to burn heretics at the stake,
For those who would church teachings forsake.

The church had supported Henry's claim,
To England's throne, and so he'd aim,
At supporting them against any move,
That tried the status quo to improve.

Very soon, Henry had hosted,
A Byzantine emperor that, he boasted,
Had a link to Rome's great imperial past,
An emperor whose dignity was vast.

Yet, despite much support, there were still,
Those in the land who desired to kill,
King Henry for being a fake and a fraud,
Saying his claim to the throne was flawed.

In the north, the Earl of Northumberland had,
Raised troops who not only in mail were clad,
But had the conviction that they rebelled,
That Henry's ambition be checked and quelled.

In battle at Shrewsbury, the armies met,
Each so determined and each so set,
On proving the right to their own cause,
To pursue the other without pause.

The Earl's brave son, Hotspur, charged,
His reputation in war already enlarged,
But here he fell doing what he loved best,
Putting himself, and his courage, to the test.

Henry's eldest son was there,
Leading, fighting and full of dare,
Until an arrow struck his face,
Wounding the prince and slowing his pace.

In Wales, rebellion also broke out,
When Owain Glyndwr raised the shout,
Of how he alone was the Prince of Wales,
With stories of rights and mystic tales.

Yet, Henry succeeded in defeating them all,
That challenged his right, and desired his fall,
Building a future for he who must follow,
To leave a sound throne, nothing hollow.

But despite all attempts, rumours persisted,
That King Richard lived and existed,
In secret places just waiting for,
The time and support to even the score.

Some even said that the Scots were involved,
Which led many people to be resolved,
To rise up against the king and his reign,
To challenge his rule again and again.

With his authority always in doubt,
With time, due to illness, for him running out,
Much of the pressure of ruling was eased,
By Henry, the son, though much had been seized.

With failing health and disease of the skin,

Which some said was leprosy due to his sin,

His rule, which many thought as unfit,

He would, in fourteen thirteen, have to quit.

Henry V
(1413-1422)

Interesting fact:

Due to his victories over France, which almost saw the unification of the two kingdoms, a strong sense of English nationalism quickly developed and blossomed, leading the way to even more conquests and the eventual rise of England as a global power.

With his father's death, young Henry took,
The mantle of King and adopted the look,
Of one who knew what a king should be,
Showing the people what they wanted to see.

A warrior king who led from the front,
Whose dynamic force would never blunt,
Showing his subjects and foes alike,
How his strength of character could easily strike.

He gained such martial skill and prowess,
When his father, the King, tried to redress,
Rebellious Wales and Englishmen who,
Thought from the king all evil grew.

He also gained much experience too,
When his father's illness steadily grew,
Leaving the King with a great need,
For his son's advancement to proceed.

Once the English throne was acquired,
Henry believed and soon aspired,
To taking back all that was lost,
In French lands, so the channel was crossed.

By fourteen fifteen, he was at war,
In a role, which to him, was never a chore,
Leading the men on another invasion,
Though many an Englishman needed persuasion.

At the Battle of Agincourt, Henry achieved,
Success which many had not believed,
Was possible in the face of the French,
Yet, his enemy's blood would Agincourt drench.

It seemed as if Henry could do no wrong,
Defeating and conquering and before long,
Paris itself, the ultimate prize,
Was beheld by Henry and his men's eyes.

In fourteen twenty, Paris was taken,
The people, and nobles, of France clearly shaken.
In the following treaty, he was declared,
Regent and future King if spared.

To wed a princess was also a part,
Of negotiations which could not fall apart,
So, Catherine of Valois was duly selected,
The French King's daughter who wasn't rejected.

All thought the nations might soon unite,
Put an end to war's fearsome blight,
But there were still those in France who thought,
This English king should always be fought.

It was while on campaign that Henry fell ill,
Yet his fighting spirit would not be still,
As he led his troops in the sweltering heat,
Clad in full armour, his foes to defeat.

Though by August of fourteen twenty-two,
Many of Henry's nobles knew,
His illness had grown to such a state,
That their king would not avoid his fate.

Catherine gave Henry a healthy boy child,
But with Henry's death, plans were compiled.
His uncle, Duke of Bedford, would supervise,
The boy's education, to teach and advise.

Henry had proven before his fall,
His skills as a general to one and all,
Whilst also showing a pious side,
His focus on war he could not hide.

Bravery and genius as a soldier showed,
Which, to his upbringing, might be owed,
But he could be cruel in certain affairs,
And often neglected his domestic cares.

Henry VI (1422-1461)

Interesting fact:

Although very young when he became King, Henry also inherited the ongoing Hundred Years War. However, he is the only English King to be also crowned as the real King of France and not just by title.

At just nine months, when he succeeded,
In acquiring the throne, unimpeded,
His mother and nobles jostled for places,
Ambition and cunning behind the faces.

He was also heir to the French throne,
Which meant this boy could one day own,
The kingdoms of France and England as well,
If intrigue and plots did not tell.

But his mother was viewed with great suspicion,
Because she was French, and so lacked permission,
To have any part in her son's upbringing,
His uncles and nobles to all power clinging.

A council of regents was created,
That English policy by them be dictated,
With the Duke of Bedford as its head,
Which meant that England, by him, was led.

But the ongoing war in France had meant,
More time in France by the Duke was spent,
With his brother, the Duke of Gloucester approved,
As regent whilst Bedford was removed.

As tutor, the Earl of Warwick was picked,
Whose teaching was firm, but not too strict,
A noble who'd serve with much loyalty,
A fitting teacher for the royalty.

Yet, Henry was still a pawn in the hands,
Of nobles who sought more wealth and lands,
Men who'd plot and scheme each day,
To gain more power and to have their say.

When Charles the seventh was duly crowned,
King of France Henry then found,
He was crowned in his own right,
King of England to his noble's delight.

Two years later in fourteen thirty-one,
Henry's position was disputed by none,
When crowned as king of France as well,
Though the title itself was just a shell.

But it wasn't until he was sixteen,
That more independence by Henry was seen,
When in fourteen thirty-seven, it was thought,
More roles as a king should be sought.

For a wife, Henry was persuaded to take,
The French King's niece with hopes to make,
England's position in France more improved,
Though the terms by many, were not approved.

Yet England had little choice but to try,
As the cost of war with France was high,
With little to show, and too much loss,
Each time the English Channel they'd cross.

Added to this, Henry was viewed,
As unfit to rule with troubles renewed,
A passive man who was pious and shy,
Who let criticism of him go by.

A circle of favourites soon arose,
Leading the King wherever they chose,
Often to serve their own ambition,
Offending others with no contrition.

Favouring peace with France and not,
A bloody war where momentum was shot,
While at home his circle of friends obtained,
More wealth from a land already drained.

Oblivious or simply not choosing to care,
The nobles and people thought it unfair,
That Henry should leave a chosen few,
To extort and rob, so rebellion grew.

Back in France, more land was taken,
By the French King, leaving England shaken,
As they saw all those gains which had been hard won,
Lost to the enemy with nothing done.

The French were aided by a holy young maid,
Joan of Arc whose great holiness stayed,
Throughout a campaign that defeated,
The English army which then retreated.

In time, just Calais on the coast remained,
The rest of the English provinces claimed,
By France, which left the English beaten,
Their words of pride humbly eaten.

Rebellion simmered near the top,
Wanting corruption by nobles to stop,
And when the king became very ill,
There was one man who could the role fill.

The Duke of York was very outspoken,
Against government he said was broken,
And with his ally, the Earl of Warwick,
Their acts would prove to be very historic.

York was named regent and would constrain,
The Queen and nobles who'd sought to reign,
Through Henry who was very unwell,
But at least was no longer under their spell.

Yet Henry's mental health became,
Better with time and so he came,
Back to the world of fast politics,
Allowing his circle to get back to their tricks.

Supported by Warwick, York could maintain,
The King was unfit because he was insane,
Stating his claim to the throne was stronger,
That Henry shouldn't rule any longer.

Tensions between the two houses grew,
Yet neither house thought nor knew,
Of what sort of war would soon develop,
How York and Lancaster would England envelope.

Each of the houses used a rose as a sign,
To rally support and get them in line.
Red for Lancaster, for York pure white,
Both very proud and keen for the fight.

At Northampton, in battle, Henry was taken,
Unharmed but defeated and somewhat shaken,
With the Queen escaping to the north,
There to raise forces, which she brought forth.

Then, at Wakefield, battle was given,
With the forces of York from the field driven,
Where much blood by both was spilled,
With York himself being killed.

By early fourteen sixty-one,

Her forces had Warwick on the run,

After he was defeated with the king liberated,

With the house of York's plans looking frustrated.

The House of York

Interesting fact:

This house was established when Edmund Langley, Edward III's fourth son, was created the 1st Duke of York.

Edward IV
(1461 – 1483)

Interesting fact:

Edward was born at Rouen in France, and whilst still young went with his father to Wales. It wasn't until he was twelve years old that he first entered London.

Though his father had not been spared,
In March the new Duke of York was declared,
King Edward the Fourth in a move to appeal,
To show that the Yorkist claim was real.

And, within six weeks, fortunes reversed,
Lancastrian forces killed or dispersed,
At the Battle of Towton, bloody and grim,
Which left the hopes of the Queen very slim.

In exile in France the Queen tried to raise,
Forces for Henry to restore those days,
When he ruled as king and she had her say,
But events were to prove that she'd had her day.

With her death in fourteen sixty-three,
The king of Scotland at last felt free,
To sue for peace with her enemies,
While Henry, still free, could do as he please.

So, in May of fourteen sixty-four,
Once more attempting to settle the score,
Henry's army, at Hexham, was soundly bested,
With Henry escaping but soon arrested.

Kept in the Tower of London that he,
Could not by supporters be quickly set free,
Henry could only sit and await,
To see how events would shape his fate.

Events and intrigue took a big twist,
Giving Henry's side a chance not missed,
When Edward and Warwick, to their dismay,
Fell out with each other and broke away.

Warwick escaped to France to find,
Henry's supporters were not far behind,
So, with theirs and France's support,
He went back to England and there Edward fought.

Edward lost and was forced to run,
His role at King seemingly done,
With Henry, once more, to his throne restored,
Though his state of health meant he was ignored.

The Earl of Warwick ruled England now,
It was to him that all had to bow,
But his role as regent would not endure,
Rule under him would not mature.

When Burgundy's lands by him were invaded,
Edward's supporters were then persuaded,
This was the time to strike and retake,
The throne and thirst for revenge to slake.

In April of fourteen seventy-one,
A major victory at Barnet was won,
By Edward and Warwick was among the slain,
With nothing to hinder Edward's reign.

In May a battle at Tewkesbury saw,
All Henry's hopes cast to the floor,
When his own son was among those killed,
The son he hoped would his dynasty build.

That day for Henry had come at great cost,
For the battle and crown were forever lost,
Leaving Edward, the master, to do as he chose,
To establish his reign as his power rose.

Henry was kept at The Tower once more,
Though fears of a rescue would only gnaw,
At Edward's mind, so he'd comply,
To political will, and Henry would die.

The next few years of Edward's rule,
Proved he was not seen as anyone's fool,
Showing a sound political sense,
In his and England's good defence.

Once more he took an English force,
Across to France upon a course,
Of conquest and hoped he might regain,
English pride and remove any stain.

But the king of France negotiated,
A deal which Edward appreciated,
Which gave the king cash and a pension,
If he agreed to the war's suspension.

In Scotland, Edward helped and backed,
A disgruntled Duke who had attacked,
The Scottish King with a hope to seize,
The throne, but the plan didn't go with ease.

Edward's brother, Richard, was sent,
Those rebellious forces to augment,
But the rebels and English failed,
When Edinburgh's castle walls weren't scaled.

Back at home, King Edward was ailing,
His health, it seemed, constantly falling,
And in April of fourteen eighty-three,
From the troubles of rule, he was set free.

His son, Prince Edward, would have to remain,
In his uncle's charge 'til he could attain,
An age when his uncle would decide,
He no longer needed his uncle as guide.

But Richard, the Duke of Gloucester, had,
A plan of his own which to some seemed bad,
Which involved the prince and the prince's brother,
That would young Edward's future smother.

Though change of fortune was not far away,
Opposition to York would have its say,
As Henry the Sixth's mother had remarried,
A Tudor whose rights to rule he carried.

Edward V
(1483)

Interesting fact:

His father laid down strict guidelines for his son's education and upbringing. His day would begin with prayers, and he wasn't allowed to stay too long in bed either. After breakfast came 'virtuous learning' followed by dinner from 10am, then listening to 'noble stories' from his tutor. Sport came in the afternoon, followed by supper served from 4pm, and the young Edward was not to be exposed to anyone who swore, fought or was an adulterer just in case he picked up any bad habits.

The Duke of Gloucester was given the care,
Of the King's son and legal heir,
That he be taught those kingly ways,
That he, as king, would receive due praise.

Richard, his uncle, was made protector,
Would act as mentor, guide, director,
But the uncle's love had already flown,
Because the uncle had plans of his own.

With his brother, Richard, Edward was taken,
To the Tower of London to awaken,
To circumstances which had changed,
To a fate his uncle had arranged.

At only twelve, Edward was young,
With coronation bells not yet rung,
As he and his younger brother were led,
From what they knew to uncertainty instead.

Their comfortable lodgings were heavily guarded,
Their royal status not quite disregarded,
As their protector ruled in their place,
To some a prince who ruled in disgrace.

With the nephews in the Tower enclosed,
Richard then had the king deposed,
By an act of Parliament, he forced through,
Whilst the plot against his nephews grew.

By this act, Richard acquired,
The title of King to which he aspired,
With Edward's followers left in no doubt,
What they, and their king, were left without.

With their uncle achieving his goals,
Many feared for the princes' souls,
And, one day, what many had feared,
Happened when the princes disappeared.

Fingers of blame were very soon pointed,
At Richard for killing God's anointed,
For having had his nephews killed,
That his own plans might be fulfilled.

Yet Richard the Third quickly denied,
Any part in the deaths, and innocence cried,
Which many people could not believe,
Though his reputation he'd try to retrieve.

Richard III
(1483-1485)

Interesting fact:

Despite later commentaries, histories and plays on Richard, which portrayed him as an evil villain, he was quite popular with nobles and the common people alike and was also a very brave and renowned soldier too.

With Edward removed, Richard could claim,
That his was the one and only name,
Which England had to recognise,
As king and rightful heir in their eyes.

Edward's parents too weren't spared,
As even their marriage had been declared,
As bigamous by Richard to lend more weight,
To his position as head of state.

This meant his brother's line could not,
Inherit the throne by his plot,
Which left king Richard free to impose,
The laws and dictates that he chose.

The Princes in the Tower weren't seen,
Which would tarnish Richard's esteem,
As people pointed the finger and said,
Richard had wanted his nephews dead.

Yet, as a king, and with ties to the north,
Richard did his best to bring forth,
Improvements to help those in need,
Where reform of government would proceed.

The Court of Requests was also approved,
That the life of the poor might be improved,
The court allowing the poor to be heard,
Where before no court would hear their word.

Even the written laws were changed,
Their use of language rearranged,
When Richard ordered they be translated,
From French to English that they be debated.

But despite attempts to do his best,
Richard's rule was put to the test,
By rebels supporting the nephew they thought,
Was still alive and for whom they fought.

Richard responded as he always did,
As he was a noble who never hid,
From the fight or those who simply dared,
To face him in battle, as he wasn't scared.

A minor rebellion occurred early on,
By the Duke of Buckingham, but the threat had gone,
But by August of fourteen eighty-five,
Rebellion, once more, was very alive.

Henry Tudor, with supporters from France,
Would face the King with sword and lance,
With a claim to the throne and so would seek,
The crown though some thought his claim was weak.

At the Battle of Bosworth, the armies met,
Where England's future would be set,
In one more fight between the factions,
York and Lancaster's bloody actions.

Henry's army was badly outnumbered,
His men, by uncertainty, likewise encumbered,
Until one of Richard's nobles changed side,
Preferring with the usurper to ride.

In a last-ditch attempt to prove his cause,
Richard charged and hacked without pause,
Getting close to where Henry, seated,
Upon his horse had not yet retreated.

But before King Richard could deliver the blow,
That would to both armies clearly show,
That his claim to the throne was truly just,
He was killed and his plan turned to dust.

As a final insult, Richard was stripped,
His armour and clothes from his body ripped,
With the corpse then carried, tied to a horse,
To Leicester and showed with little remorse.

With no one willing to speak or praise,
Richard's rule came under the gaze,
Of every critic who was eager to please,
The Tudor king, which they did with ease.

Accused of murder and vilified,
The image of Richard was simplified,
Into one who was evil, corrupt and base,
As the victor of Bosworth gave him a new face.

The Tudors

Interesting fact:

The dynasty which ruled England originated from a marriage between a Tudor noble from North Wales and the daughter of the King of France.

Henry VII
(1485 – 1509)

Interesting fact:

Henry was a King who realised that good rule and leadership needed good financial security, so he introduced several economic and diplomatic ideas to help restore and improve England's financial situation.

Henry would have to work very hard,

If his reign was not to be marred,

With threats from those he had defeated,

So, policies would be completed.

He'd need to secure his power base,

If he was to prevent public disgrace,

And needed to make good decisions,

To prevent his realm from having divisions.

Henry honoured the pledge he'd conveyed,

That the bond of the houses wouldn't fade,

So, Elizabeth of York soon became,

His queen so's not dissent to inflame.

To cement the two houses further still,

And the peace of the land to fulfil,

The emblem for his reign he chose,

Was the red of Lancaster, and York's white rose.

Two roses combined as red and white,

Hoping, at last, to end that fight,

Which had swept the land like an evil plague,

Its cause, for most, both wasteful and vague.

If Henry could settle his troubled nation,

Secure his dynasty's recent foundation,

Then perhaps he might the people enrol,

In making the nation wealthy and whole.

France was always a problem nearby,

Which every king of England would try,

To keep in mind and keep in check,

That plans of France wouldn't peace wreck.

For France was always seeking new gains,

Trying to cause new problems and pains,

Always seeking new ways to expand,

That forced the English to make a stand.

Yet bloody wars were always expensive,
The loss of revenue always extensive,
So, Henry advanced to longed for peace,
That his loss of wealth might finally cease.

France recognised Henry's position,
Helping Henry's political condition,
Enabling the king to fill his coffers,
Disarming his critics, his detractors, and scoffers.

While Scotland was still a political concern,
And to this problem Henry would turn.
He betrothed his daughter to James the Fourth,
Packing her off to the realm in the north.

Henry was courting more power and prestige,
Fearful lest some would his nation besiege.
He knew the value of a sound reputation,
The work that was needed to see aspiration.

With years spent in poverty, a lesson was learned,

Creating in him a passion which burned,

Giving the king a lifelong desire,

To never be poor, and from this never tire.

With a mind that was set to build freer trade,

With competent officials great profit was made.

His hoarding of wealth would make many moan,

But the seeds of greatness were carefully sown.

Reforming the currency, Henry would join,

With men of learning to improve English coin.

Determined to show his concern he was willing,

To make many changes and produced the first shilling.

Known for sound administration,

His dynasty gained a good foundation.

Knowing he should never let,

His house fall into ruinous debt.

With that in mind, he was apprised,

That plans for prosperity weren't capsized.

Building his and his nation's wealth,

By cunning, intelligence and political stealth.

Over the years, his position improved,

As fears of the dynasty were slowly removed.

And one of the ways to show his intent,

Was producing a son, an heir to present.

Every new monarch clearly knew,

How the wind of politics clearly blew,

And how some nobles might try to claim,

That their house had a royal name.

Henry needed to secure his place,

By giving the people an heir to embrace,

Helping the people to see and admit,

That the house of Tudor to rule was fit.

Giving the nation a boy and an heir,
Would help reduce any worry or care,
That civil war wouldn't rise yet again,
That families wouldn't feel that pain.

When Arthur was born, the boy was named,
Heir to the throne, and duly proclaimed,
The one who'd inherit everything,
To make any doubting opinions swing.

Arthur would grow to become a young man,
Hopefully fulfilling his father's plan,
That would see young Arthur one day succeed,
To becoming the King so the line might proceed.

So, Arthur was schooled by the best there were,
That kingly virtue might within him stir.
Taught by the best that the age could give,
That the house of Tudor, through him, would live.

Wishing for England to be closer to Spain,
That France's ambitions might work in vain,
To Catherine of Aragon Arthur was wed,
And English and Spanish friendship was spread.

With Arthur, the dynasty felt much pride,
And Henry himself found it hard to hide,
The fact that he saw in his first-born son,
The Tudor succession would continue to run.

Yet tragedy upon their house descended,
With illness to which they were undefended,
Taking young Arthur whilst still very young,
As marriage songs were still being sung.

The death of young Arthur broke Henry's heart,
Temporarily pulling his plans all apart.
But Henry had had an heir and a spare,
And Henry, his son, who would the crown bear.

Young Henry had lived a different life,
Hadn't learnt the ways of political strife.
Some thought he hadn't the wherewithal,
But rose to the challenge and destiny's call.

Young, Handsome and very athletic,
Musician, strong and very poetic,
Henry was healthy and full of passion,
Who liked modernity and modern fashion.

Suddenly, Henry would have to adjust,
When into the centre of attention thrust,
Told he'd have to ready himself,
And not remain on politics shelf.

The king had insisted that Arthur's young bride,
Should stay in England and at court abide,
Hoping to make a match that was new,
That alliance with Spain should still go through.

Henry would reign for a few years longer,

His plans for England growing stronger,

Making his nation rich and secure,

A Tudor dynasty that would live and endure.

But then in fifteen hundred and nine,

There came the end of the first in his line.

At the age of fifty-two he died,

His legacy to England now well fortified.

Henry VIII (1509 – 1547)

Interesting fact:

The king realised he could use something called 'bill of attainder' with which to punish those he suspected of plotting against him. By using this method, it denied the accused any proper legal process and allowed Henry to confiscate all of their wealth.

Only seventeen when he ascended the throne,

Henry's court would set the tone,

Of the Renaissance which he held dear,

Giving rise to the love of a new idea.

An intelligent man who was gifted, complex,

Determined to be master of his subjects.

Driven to rule by God's divine right,

With nothing allowed to challenge his might.

At the end of the long medieval age,

Henry turned the Renaissance page,

Welcoming thoughts that were embracing,

New ideas that seemed worth chasing.

Young Henry and Catherine were soon betrothed,

Both in stately apparel clothed,

Not married for politics, but shortly to find,

Love for each other in body and mind.

With his queen by his side, he would display,
An extravagant court, with a vast array,
Of courtiers and pageant which would impress,
By its dances and feasts which went to excess.

Young and in love, both he and she,
Would entertain, and all would see,
Their happiness and how they spent their time,
Delighting in music and the love poem's rhyme.

He loved to read, and had a thousand books,
His sense of fashion gained a thousand looks.
His faith in God helped him to cope,
Made defender of the faith by the Pope.

Sport was something he couldn't ignore,
With a love of jousting deep in his core.
Clad in armour upon his steed,
Chivalry and glory were his need.

Playing tennis where many learnt,
Pride and skill were often burnt,
With Henry showing an ability,
That only confirmed his virility.

For many years by his side,
His young and beautiful Spanish bride,
Would do her best to present,
A son to succeed who was heaven sent.

Through years of marriage, children were born,
Then from loving arms most were torn,
Taken by illness and disease,
Bringing the parents to their knees.

One did survive who was a girl,
Who was, for a while, her father's pearl,
Named Mary she'd live and survive the rest,
But a son would be what the king thought best.

Young King Henry tried to maintain,

A regal image and so attain,

A look of power to Spain and France,

His reputation to enhance.

He also arranged the new formation,

Of English and Welsh unification,

Binding the two as a modern state,

That would a greater nation create.

War with France was always a fear,

Yet young Henry tried to appear,

Strong and determined not to give in,

Not deterred by the battle's din.

At the Battle of the Spurs, in fifteen thirteen,

Henry's prowess as leader was clearly seen,

When the French army by his was defeated,

Losing the day and sadly retreated.

At home, Queen Catherine had to contend,
With a Scottish invasion and was forced to defend,
Those lands in the north which were under threat,
Defeating the Scots when much blood was let.

The Battle of Flodden was a crushing blow,
To Scottish ambition, and would clearly show,
That Catherine and Henry, together, worked well,
And in their marriage union would dwell.

Later, to resolve any rivalry,
And in a great show of chivalry,
King Henry of England had agreed,
A peaceful mission to France to lead.

Henry would his courtiers assemble,
Not clad in armour to make the French tremble,
But with all the trappings of love and peace,
That more understanding might increase.

Meeting King Francis with tact and guile,
Arriving in splendid, magnificent style,
Henry and Francis stood tall and bold,
Equals in the Field of the Cloth of Gold.

This extravagant show and mighty display,
Of national prowess and kingly array,
Brought them together and was there to present,
Those bonds with each other to further cement.

But foreign diplomacy would shortly break,
The hopes and dreams that were at stake,
When Cardinal Wolsey, Henry's right hand,
Gave the realm a different stand.

For Wolsey had with Spain arranged,
An alliance making France estranged.
When Spain and France their war began,
France's old hatred for England then ran.

The idea of a son was what Henry revered,
And the lack of an heir he deeply feared.
The King's Great Matter would only convince,
Henry's court that he needed a prince.

Henry and Catherine had tried for so long,
To give the news to the waiting throng,
That a son was born who'd live to be,
The Tudor dynasty's guarantee.

This desire for a son was a driving force,
Which would lead Henry on a darker course,
For as his queen grew older in years,
Conception grew rarer, which played on his fears.

But one day his eye caught sight of a maid,
Whose lure and attraction would not quickly fade.
He wanted this woman like no other,
Desired to make her his brand new lover.

Anne Boleyn was her name,

Full of spirit he couldn't tame.

He did his best to woo and entice,

To draw her in to his lust and vice.

Anne refused to be any part,

Of a simple affair, and fought from the start,

Telling the king she wanted more,

Than to be used like a common whore.

She promised the king that from her womb,

A son would be born which he could groom,

To be his heir and fulfil his dream,

But only as queen would she Henry redeem.

Anne had lived at the French court,

Where love and politics had been taught.

In the ways of seduction, she was skilled,

And soon King Henry with lust was filled.

Henry's wife had clearly detected,
Her husband's obsession which she suspected,
Was not like any he'd had in the past,
Which were intense but would never last.

But Henry was keen to have this maid,
Who showed she was cunning and not afraid.
Wolsey was sent to the Pope to secure,
A deal that made the marriage impure.

But the Pope would not grant a dispensation,
Leaving King Henry in bitter frustration.
Wolsey was blamed for failing to gain,
A legal release from his longing and pain.

Wolsey's fall from grace was cruel and swift,
Even when he gave Hampton Court as a gift.
Henry wanted some poor soul to blame,
With Wolsey the man his enemies would name.

At Hampton Court, both Spain and France,
Each in turn were given the chance,
To see for themselves Henry's strength,
To enjoy his company at great length.

With Wolsey no longer in splendour and style,
Henry's treatment was very hostile.
Yet a man filled the space whose genius would tell,
An excellent administrator called Thomas Cromwell.

He became one of Henry's closest advisers,
Aware of his problem, and a great sympathiser.
Cromwell would help to open the way,
For the king to divorce and have his say.

Yet, the king would need to break from Rome,
For Henry to have what he wanted at home.
Then Cromwell used the king's frustration,
To enhance the Protestant reformation.

In time, the king was made to see,
What wealth and power he'd have if free,
From all the influence the Pope exerted,
If the catholic church could be deserted.

Anne helped to play a significant part,
Using her charms and her subtle art,
In convincing the king of the protestant cause,
Which Henry welcomed with sound applause.

Breaking from Rome, the king declared,
He would do the thing which he had dared,
Divorcing his wife and marrying Anne,
Finally seeing the fruit of his plan.

In the Act of Supremacy, which quickly followed,
A change in religion would have to be swallowed,
By all his subjects, whatever their standing,
Or suffer the punishment and its branding.

Belief was real for rich and poor,
Their faith in God went to the core,
Helping each soul to truly ascend,
To see God's face and sins amend.

Suddenly, Henry wanted to change,
To beliefs which were alien, new and strange.
His people would have to be humble and meek,
The spirit and will of God to seek.

The Pope excommunicated Henry and those,
Who followed his plan and heresy chose.
But the act of the Pope Henry dismissed,
Now he had all he wanted clutched in his fist.

With Henry declared as the head of the church,
The people would have their conscience to search.
No more could they seek the Pope's distant blessing,
With the change considered new and distressing.

For failure to acknowledge Henry as head,
Left many arrested, and many left dead.
Henry's old friend, Sir Thomas More,
Wouldn't swear allegiance and was soon done for.

With Henry the church would be reformed,
Different devotions to God were performed.
Mass in English was soon introduced,
And an English Bible would be produced.

While up in the north, most still retained,
Love of the old church, and faith still remained.
Angry and sad at faith's new revision,
They knew their belief was on a collision.

But the king was happy, or at least for a while,
Assured he'd be greeted by a son's happy smile.
When Anne gave birth to a girl, not a boy,
Henry was stripped of contentment and joy.

For many long years, Henry had waited,

To marry his love, and by promises baited.

The birth of a girl stole some magic away,

With the question of inheritance once more at play.

Named Elizabeth, this girl would one day find,

Her place in history clearly defined,

But, for now, she wasn't essential,

As the king desired an heir's great potential.

Try as he might, he hadn't acquired,

The birth of a son which he strongly desired.

He knew that there was much at stake,

And believed it was Anne's sole mistake.

Try as they would, they could not achieve,

The son which they sought, and Anne to retrieve,

The place in Henry's fleeting affections,

And a miscarriage followed despite rigorous inspections.

Yet, Henry's affections for Anne were slipping,
The scales against her position tipping,
Ironically turning to a Lady in Waiting,
A position Anne held when believed captivating.

The lady in question was Jane Seymour,
Into whose arms his affections would pour.
Beautiful, affectionate, and full of charm,
Her attributes would the king disarm.

Anne never played the submissive role,
Not to be subservient her ultimate goal.
She was a woman full of great intellect,
Which Henry enjoyed and showed respect.

But their marriage with argument was often filled,
Which, by degrees, their love slowly killed.
Gone was the magic of Henry's obsession,
Now that he had her as his sole possession.

His desire for Jane was obvious and true,
Which the court could see and many now knew,
Would mean the end of Anne's mighty grip,
Upon the king, and her power would slip.

Believing his marriage cursed and doomed,
The spectre of ruin over Anne loomed.
Seeing her status beginning to crumble,
Courtiers were heard to whisper and mumble.

Her fall was rapid, but Anne wouldn't cower,
Even when she was taken to live in the Tower.
All of the charges she quickly denied,
But of treason and adultery Anne would be tried.

Henry was set on marrying Jane,
A fact which the king made simple and plain.
He arranged for Anne to be beheaded,
That his new hope might be quickly wedded.

Married within a week of Anne's death,

Jane gave Henry new life and new breath.

The king had found a lover to cherish,

A joy in life he believed wouldn't perish.

Henry's joy was magnified many fold,

When, by Jane, he was told,

She was pregnant, and hopes ran high,

That Jane would his longing at last satisfy.

And still the Reformation progressed,

Some feeling punished, some feeling blessed.

Henry and Cromwell avidly pursued,

Reforms which the Catholics found base and crude.

Then northern counties openly rebelled,

Their mass of numbers not being repelled.

Southwards they marched to demonstrate,

Against the reforms and their church's fate.

Henry told the leaders he'd hear their petition,
Ignoring this open act of sedition.
But when the mighty force was dispersed,
His sympathetic show was reversed.

Jane was aware how the rebels felt,
Begged to make Henry's fury melt,
Yet dozens of men were not exempted,
For the threat to Henry they'd attempted.

With any rebellion brutally crushed,
Henry now saw the reforms should be rushed.
Dismantling the popish threat forever,
And finishing his great religious endeavour.

The Thirty-Nine Articles of religious reform,
Would, for religion, become the norm,
Along with the Book of Common Prayer,
And those who rebelled would have to beware.

Soon after the king had a happy distraction,
When Jane had her first birthing contraction.
Delighted and hopeful that at last he'd find,
The joy of a son by God designed.

Jane gave the king the son he'd been seeking,
That prize of which for years he'd been speaking.
But Jane had a fever, and she was ill,
And this would Henry's true love kill.

By the death of poor Jane, the king was distraught,
While the touch of his son helped the dark thought.
With gain and loss, he was happy and sad,
Though Cromwell knew there was more to be had.

Cromwell had a plan in motion,
To secure the protestant faith's promotion,
By marrying Henry to a German princess,
Whose beauty, he said, would all ills redress.

Henry would marry Anne of Cleves,
Among celebrations and festivities,
Hoping he'd find another soul mate,
To do his duty for people and state.

Yet, Henry had felt an instant distaste,
To the German woman he suddenly faced.
Perhaps still mourning his Jane and her smile,
Or the way Anne would speak and her German style.

Whatever the reason, Henry refused,
To consummate the marriage, and wouldn't be used,
In political ties when he wanted affection,
And the 'Flanders Mare' never got much inspection.

In an act that seemed very indulgent,
Their marriage received a happy annulment.
Anne was given a house and a pension,
And Henry was happy to be free of the tension.

At court, she'd be an honoured guest,
'The King's beloved sister' addressed.
She'd spend her days in dignified existence,
With the king's approval and gracious assistance.

But, as for Cromwell, things would get worse,
As Henry began his name to curse,
For enemies of Cromwell eagerly spoke,
Of his failure and revenge awoke.

Enemies in Council wasted no time,
In having him sent to the prison's grime.
Locked in the tower on charges of treason,
Born out of jealousy and hateful reason.

Now the Council had the master's ear,
And with Cromwell in prison they need not fear,
The genius, which was now not in favour,
Then worked on the king lest he should waver.

These Council members went to the extreme,

That they might deliver their own special scheme.

With the Duke of Norfolk at its head,

They'd try to influence the king instead.

The duke had a niece called Catherine Howard,

Who, through the king, made the duke empowered,

To have more influence in power dealing,

Convinced his influence was more appealing.

Yet, without a hearing or even a trial,

In an act which was cruel, unjust and vile,

Cromwell was taken to Tower Hill,

Where a botched beheading laid him still.

Later, Henry would sadly lament,

The servant who'd shown such good intent.

Condemning those who showed they were glad,

Henry lost the best servant he ever had.

The Duke of Norfolk found Catherine a place,
In Anne of Cleves court to show her face.
Pretty, lively, and very young,
Words of her virtue to Henry were sung.

Norfolk hoped that with an attraction,
He'd gain much favour for his faction,
Which hoped that Henry might be returned,
To the Catholic faith for which the duke yearned.

By now, Henry's zeal in reform was cooling,
Imbued, as he was, in traditional schooling.
Traditional values of religion were sought,
That extreme reformers might be fought.

By what he'd released, the king was alarmed,
Though by some of the changes Henry was charmed.
Through all of division, they would have to sift,
Though to conservatism Henry would drift.

But, as Henry's favour for Catherine grew,
The king began to hope and view,
The pretty young girl as a future wife,
To give new lease to his weary life.

With Henry's attraction, came Norfolk's rise,
As the king saw Catherine through lover's eyes.
The recent annulment meant he could choose,
And Catherine would surely entertain and amuse.

Henry's heart was captivated,
His longing for love now satiated.
He saw in her a vivacious youth,
A carefree life with innocent truth.

In fifteen forty, they said their vows,
Then, in love's embrace, would carouse,
Lost in their joy of wedded bliss,
Drunk by love's true gentle kiss.

Catherine was young and would often behave,
With innocent charm and would Henry enslave.
Only a child when she became,
The queen who could his temper tame.

Yet, her life for the role was not prepared,
And her joy of life she would have shared,
With those in the court who felt as she,
Who enjoyed the pleasures of a reveller's spree.

With Catherine the king felt fresh new life,
Which melted away his pain and strife.
Her youth and innocent carefree ways,
Took Henry back to his youthful days.

He saw in her a youth which was lost,
Warming his heart that was touched by frost.
He bathed in that warmth and rejuvenation,
Feeling much love and appreciation.

He'd heard of rumours of Catherine's misdeeds,
But dismissed them all to assuage his needs.
He wanted his 'Rose without a Thorn',
So, a mask of denial by him was worn.

With Henry overweight and crippled too,
Catherine's desire for a lover grew.
A boy she'd loved some time before,
To whom much love she'd given, swore.

Naive, tactless and very reckless,
Her plans for liaisons were often feckless.
But the court of Henry had men to advise,
And word got to Henry by trusted spies.

Charged with adultery, which Henry detested,
Catherine Howard was duly arrested.
When, to the Tower, she was sent,
Her seventeen months as queen were spent.

Henry's heart was brutally crushed,
Once his Catherine had been hushed.
In her he'd seen all life's appeal,
Yet now all life didn't seem so real.

The sudden fall of his queen was a shock,
And into depression his mind would lock.
Tormented by longing, he often wept,
As into his thoughts the memories crept.

Henry was old, and courtiers conceded,
That now a new wife was not really needed.
But Henry still needed to try and find,
A woman to love who was caring and kind.

Jane Seymour's brother was courting a lady,
Whose reputation offered safety,
From all those troubles he'd sought to avoid,
From women whose ways had hopes all destroyed.

He saw in the bearing of Catherine Parr,
A woman whose care might take them far,
Along the path that was quiet and calm,
And would give old Henry much needed balm.

Catherine was clever, and well educated,
Her skills in languages well demonstrated.
A keen reformist, she would often debate,
Outspoken views which would vex and frustrate.

Yet Henry clearly saw in her,
A draw which would love's passions stir.
And in July, fifteen forty-three,
Their marriage became reality.

Despite his age, Henry still made war,
Taking the fight to France's door.
But before the war with France was launched,
Scotland's ambition would have to be staunched.

At the Battle of Solway Moss,
Scotland suffered another loss,
But this was far from her leader's undoing,
And the years of war were called the 'Rough Wooing'.

In France the king eventually took,
Boulogne which his cannon bombarded and shook.
But Henry's allies made a separate peace,
While Henry's fight with France wouldn't cease.

Then in fifteen forty-five,
France's navy would arrive,
Off the coast near the Isle of Wight,
Causing alarm when they came in sight.

A permanent navy by Henry was shaped,
The Tudor Rose upon them draped,
That England might not fall to those,
Who war and invasion often chose.

The night before battle, Henry dined,
Aboard the Great Harry, where he assigned,
Sir George Carew to face the French,
And victory from his foes to wrench.

So, Henry's fleet went out to engage,
To deliver the King's indignant rage,
That the French would dare to try and trespass,
And English valour try to surpass.

The Mary Rose was there to show,
That France's attempt would be laid low.
Her decks were bristling with many guns,
Adding to her many tons.

Hundreds of men crowded her decks,
Keen to turn the French ships to wrecks.
But when she turned, all were surprised,
When the mighty ship quickly capsized.

Meanwhile, his trust in his wife matured,
To the point where Henry was assured,
That Catherine could rule while he was away,
Acting as Regent and England's mainstay.

Catherine was only thirty-one,
But she couldn't give Henry another son.
Attentive, intelligent, loving not wild,
Alas she couldn't give her husband a child.

Yet, she did her best to care and nurse,
The ageing Henry whose condition got worse.
Overindulgence and a leg full of sores,
Left the king in bed giving her the state chores.

Though Catherine tried to do as he bid,
From Henry's affections she almost slid,
When a conversation with him grew heated,
When he, by heresy, by her was greeted.

A religious question by them was debated,

With Catherine's knowledge on faith illustrated.

King Henry was angry, ordering Catherine's arrest,

But she acted with penitence, putting fears to rest.

Catherine would stay by Henry's side,

A devoted wife until he died.

And in January of fifteen forty-seven,

The troubled King Henry went to Jane in heaven.

Edward VI (1547 – 1553)

Interesting Fact:

Edward was the first ever English monarch to be raised as a protestant, and even went so far as to have his catholic sister, Mary, removed from the line of succession in favour of his protestant first cousin, Lady Jane Grey.

Henry's son, Edward, was next in line,
Receiving the throne when just aged nine.
Jane Seymour was the one who'd given birth,
To the child the king believed had worth,

Only a son could give him what he craved,
That his line of succession would be paved.
Daughters to Henry weren't worth very much,
Believing them weak with their feminine touch.

So, when his son eventually came,
Henry had not the slightest shame,
In showing his boy more favour and love,
Believing this boy was from God up above.

He gave young Edward the very best,
And in his attentions, he wouldn't rest,
Making sure his prince had it all,
That one day his son as king would stand tall.

The finest scholars for him were provided,
That Edward to his role would be guided.
Titles, houses and the best food,
So, Edward's destiny might be pursued.

Intellectually very precocious,
His religious zeal was also ferocious.
Still a young boy when he gained the throne,
Henry arranged he'd not rule alone.

From his birth, he was never strong,
Though doctors managed his life to prolong,
Until the day he became their king,
And with-it future's hope to bring.

The plan was set that a council of Lords,
Would guide the boy slowly towards,
The day when Edward was old enough,
To rule alone and was wise and tough.

So, the Duke of Somerset took command,
Edward's uncle who would demand,
That he alone should rule the realm,
As the only man who could take the helm.

He became the nation's main director,
Styling himself as their Protector.
In Edward Seymour power would rest,
While many believed they were being oppressed.

A zealous protestant, who would purify,
England's religion by rules he'd apply.
He issued the Book of Common Prayer,
Supported by Edward who was in his care.

Within a short time, rebellion followed,
Angry that more reform should be swallowed.
The Earl of Warwick was sent to defeat,
Those who dared with reform to compete.

But the Earl of Warwick, once he had succeeded,
In defeating rebellion now knew what was needed,
And soon The Protector's position had crumbled,
His power gone; his arrogance humbled.

The Earl of Warwick now stepped in,
Not claiming Protector, but the veil was thin.
Protestant reform was keenly stepped up,
With all now forced to drink from its cup.

With Edward's applause and sound approval,
Protestant doctrine saw the removal,
Of anything which of popery consisted,
While people were punished if they resisted.

Promoted to the Duke of Northumberland,
This powerful man for his cause would stand,
Convincing the king they'd have to work fast,
If their protestant ways were to ever last.

Fifteen fifty-two and the Prayer Book became,

The means by which they'd heresy tame.

Or so they hoped as idols were smashed,

As Catholic imagery was brutally trashed.

Yet, whatever plans Northumberland had,

It began to unravel and began to go bad,

When Edward became ill and began to fade,

Though all of England for recovery preyed.

The doctors could see the king wouldn't live,

Telling Edward to ask God to forgive,

Any transgressions and any sin,

That a place in heaven he might one day win.

But even now Northumberland moved,

Getting Edward to favour a plan he approved,

Which altered the order of succession,

In a last great act of protestant expression.

For Edward knew that his sister Mary,
If gaining the throne, would try to bury,
All his reforms and soundly stick,
To her beliefs as a Catholic.

He believed that Mary would stop his reform,
Take the nation through religious storm,
Bringing the people back to Rome,
Whilst causing division in every home.

Declared illegitimate, Mary would not,
Be able to change or work to plot,
The overthrow of Edward's attempt,
To make reforms, rousing her contempt.

Lady Jane Grey, would be submitted,
As queen in her place and would be pitted,
Against Mary Tudor if she should resist,
Or for her legal accession insist.

Henry the Seventh's great granddaughter,
Her appointment as Queen would unleash slaughter,
As Jane and Mary's supporters engaged,
With all by the challenge soon enraged.

Jane was Northumberland's daughter in law,
And the Duke believed she was in his claw,
Where he'd have control of this innocent girl,
As he let his sinister pan unfurl.

In July of fifteen fifty-three,
Northumberland and his house would see,
Just how far Mary would go,
When Edward died and his plan would flow.

Jane was thought to be a mere pawn,
An innocent girl from which could be drawn,
All Northumberland chose to dictate,
That would seal Mary's wicked fate.

But Mary was of Henry's stock,
And to her banner a host would flock,
So, when Northumberland's navy rebelled,
Mary's forces quickly swelled.

In just a few days, Northumberland's threat,
By Mary Tudor's forces were met.
As public support was at Mary's root,
To whom all rights they'd attribute.

Mary's resolve had been soundly tested,
But all her foes had been quickly bested,
Leaving her right as queen undisputed,
Her legitimate role as queen unpolluted.

Mary I

(1553 – 1558)

Interesting Fact:

Mary was the first real female monarch to rule in her own right. However, many despised and feared her due to her determination to restore the nation to the Catholic faith. She had almost 300 people burnt at the stake for not conforming to her wishes.

As a child, Mary was close to her mother,
And soon Queen Catherine would discover,
That Mary was also intellectually bright,
Who, for knowledge, had an appetite.

As sole heir, for a time all considered,
That Mary, as queen, would be delivered,
Upon the throne taking her place,
With royal powers and regal grace.

When young, she would quickly find,
How her future was designed,
By her father's desire to marry her to,
Some princes where hopeful alliance drew.

It soon was clear that Mary's face,
Was to help build Henry's power base,
A potential bride to some foreign pact,
Which, by marriage, would be backed.

Yet, suitors came and then they retired,
When diplomatic talks expired,
Leaving Mary as a possible pawn,
When Henry's foreign plans were drawn.

Remaining unmarried all the while,
Well versed in the arts of a lady, gentile,
Her religious fervour she keenly embraced,
A belief which Mary would not see erased.

For her mother brought her up to believe,
That she should God's kind grace perceive,
Through staying faithful to her belief,
Regardless of mere mortal grief.

But when her father gained his divorce,
Mary's status lost its force,
Finding herself cruelly claimed,
As illegitimate, her position shamed.

Stripped of her title of England's princess,
Longing for all her ills to redress,
Mary found comfort in the faith she had,
Doing her duty, though angry and sad.

Fearing that Anne sought her execution,
The fear never broke Mary's resolution,
Not to admit to her illegitimate role,
Refusing the convent, though Anne would cajole.

When Anne fell from grace with Henry's displeasure,
She gained better status, a house and more leisure,
To contemplate just where she now stood,
And to bend in the wind for her livelihood.

For Henry asked Mary to see and admit,
That his marriage to Catherine hadn't been fit,
Which is why with a son they hadn't been blessed,
To which young Mary, grudgingly, confessed.

When Edward was born, she was selected,
As the Prince's godmother, being so well respected.
Though plain in looks, she was a popular figure,
Her reputation just getting bigger.

Yet the title of bastard was still well attached,
Though plans for marriage were often hatched.
Princes came forward, but all the plans failed,
With her and her father's plans derailed.

Only when Henry married Catherine Howard,
And the king's new life blossomed and flowered,
Was Mary allowed back to the court,
To see the new couple play and cavort.

Then in fifteen forty-four,
An act was passed which would not ignore,
Mary's status and she was declared,
Successor to Edward if by death she were spared.

Yet when young Edward had taken his place,
And protestant reform gained apace,
Once more the princess was in danger's way,
Fearing her brother's zealous array.

She continued to celebrate the Catholic mass,
And with her brother reached an impasse,
Who thought his sister was desperately wrong,
Whose heresy was treason and dangerously strong.

But Edward was ill, and wouldn't survive,
To see his plans in England thrive.
Though Lady Jane Grey was named by him,
As the next in line, making Mary's hopes grim.

Acting quickly, Mary was forced,
To raise an army, and war was endorsed.
In just a few weeks, rebel forces were routed,
Paying the price for her dignity flouted.

In October of fifteen fifty-three,

The Bishop of Winchester would oversee,

Mary's longed for coronation,

To much rejoicing and sensation.

For being a queen in her own right,

Not appointed by marriage or king's delight,

The first proper queen to have all dominion,

Gaining the throne by right not opinion.

But Mary's heart quickly yearned,

For the old religion which her father had spurned.

Protestant power was quickly undone,

As the Catholic creed was rapidly spun.

To show the people her intentions were clear,

Mary would to the Spanish steer,

When a marriage to Philip would be ventured,

An alliance with Spain's mighty empire entered.

Those of her nobles who'd gathered much,
During reform, now feared the touch,
Of old Catholicism, and what it would mean,
And hoped that they could intervene.

But Mary was set to take them all back,
To the old religion, and get them on track,
So that England, again, might be in the fold,
With Papal approval and not in the cold.

'My marriage is my own affair',
Mary was heard to loudly declare,
Chastising her lords and Parliament too,
From where dissent and rebellion grew.

A protestant rebellion quickly broke out,
With Sir Thomas Wyatt's rebellious shout,
Encouraging those who sought to remain,
With the protestant church, and reform to attain.

Yet, Wyatt was beaten, and Mary would marry,
More determined than ever that she would carry,
England back from the vile and depraved,
That the path to heaven by her would be paved.

Her sister Elizabeth was implicated,
In Wyatt's rebellion and soon located,
In the Tower, but nothing was proved,
So then to house arrest was removed.

Questioned for days, Elizabeth said,
She was loyal to Mary, but rumours were fed,
Putting the princess in a situation,
Defenceless to every accusation.

The laws of heresy were revived,
As she and Philip continually strived,
To punish those who would not recant,
Who would not heretical ways supplant.

Mary had often said and insisted,
That violent punishment should be resisted.
But for those who chose to remain estranged,
A gruesome death would be arranged.

Many would suffer for religion's sake,
Becoming a martyr when burnt at the stake.
Encouraged by a fanatical zeal,
Many would Mary's intolerance feel.

On gaining the throne, people had cheered,
Yet now the queen was hated and feared.
She and Philip were loathed and reviled,
As people to their martyrdoms filed.

Mary hoped that a son would help to appease,
Growing dissent, and would help her to please,
Her people who now longed for an end,
To her bloody rule and the zealous trend.

Though Mary would not easily find,
A child in her womb, or peace in her mind,
For she didn't conceive, though her stomach swelled,
A phantom pregnancy, with joy withheld.

When war with France was again renewed,
Her councillor's views were dismissed and subdued.
A war that went bad which against her would weigh,
When the English forces lost the port of Calais.

Her love for Philip was shown as sincere,
Though the Spanish king would rarely be near.
Grieving and childless, the queen became ill,
A sorrow which only her faith could fill.

Eventually, Mary's wrath relented,
And to her sister she consented,
To make Elizabeth the one to succeed,
If a child of her own did not precede.

In November of fifteen fifty-eight,

Mary was dying and lay prostrate.

A reign begun with hopes so high,

Ending with people wishing she'd die.

Elizabeth I (1558 – 1603)

Interesting Fact:

By the end of her reign, Elizabeth was considered to be one of the best educated women of her age. She could speak French, Italian, Spanish and Dutch as well as the more native Welsh, Scottish, Cornish and Irish languages.

On September seventh, fifteen thirty-three,

Henry's hopes would fall to debris,

When Anne Boleyn, to a girl, gave birth,

Which wasn't to Henry's hope or mirth.

Yet, the girl seemed healthy and was alive,

And both her parents hoped she would thrive,

To grow into a lady of bearing,

Full of wisdom, learning, grace and caring.

But when Elizabeth was still very small,

Her mother, from power, would quickly fall.

Her father's affections were then redirected,

When Elizabeth's mother, for death, was selected.

Declared illegitimate, the princess was dropped,

From the right of succession, her privileges cropped.

When Edward was born, she was made to attend,

In the prince's house to serve and befriend.

Though her own education had not been neglected,
As education and learning by her were expected.
In time, young Elizabeth definitely showed,
That intellect and wisdom through her flowed.

Mastering languages like Latin and Greek,
Elizabeth's intelligence would often seek,
To push the boundaries of learning and thought,
As the wonder of learning within her was caught.

Intelligent teachers to her were assigned,
That the Princess Elizabeth might one day find,
The joy of a book, and all it can teach,
That she, one day, might enlightenment reach.

Elizabeth's joy in continued education,
Was a blessing to her and also the nation.
To further her knowledge was all she desired,
Making Elizabeth formidable, and greatly admired.

In fifteen fifty-eight, at the age of twenty-five,

Elizabeth was queen, and hope would revive,

For a monarch who was fertile and very young,

So, songs of joy for the future were sung.

On the eve of Elizabeth's coronation,

People watched in adoration,

As Elizabeth rode along the street,

Gladly responding to the people she'd meet.

The people were happy to view her procession,

Encouraged by her regal impression.

Also encouraged by her religious creed,

They saw in her reign hope's future seed.

No more the threat of a catholic alliance,

No more the catholic religious compliance,

As everyone hoped Elizabeth's belief,

Would not cause them harm, worry or grief.

Though the queen was always wise and pragmatic,

She hated things that might be schismatic,

Fearing the puritans who wanted more,

She embraced some catholic traits under law.

With the monarch as head, a solution was found,

A settlement, they hoped, would grievances ground.

Some catholic traits were willingly kept,

That her people might hopefully changes accept.

The queen would become governor supreme,

Furthering her brother's and father's dream,

Of making the monarch the church's head,

An image of Elizabeth's leadership bred.

Government officials would be asked to swear,

That she was supreme in worship and prayer.

While heresy laws were quickly repealed,

An act which to most were right and appealed.

Yet, forefront in Elizabeth's mind,
Was to look to her nobles and somehow find,
A council who could help with her task,
Of ruling the nation and opinion ask.

William Cecil was chief of them all,
Upon which Elizabeth would often call,
To advise her of steps she would have to take,
Helping with policies she'd have to make.

For forty years he was by her side,
Her faith in his wisdom she'd never hide.
For both were rarely caught unawares,
Trying to avoid political snares.

To Elizabeth's reign he was devoted,
Receiving gifts and with titles promoted.
He did his best to make her rule thrive,
Serving her well while he was alive.

Yet, he also found it hard to adjust,

When new ideas upon him were thrust,

Finding it hard to use and write,

In Arabic numbers which had come to light.

Cecil would always try to conduct,

His Queen over obstacles which sought to obstruct.

Wary of others with new thought or theme,

Which Cecil feared might upset the regime.

And, as a woman, her people expected,

That a suitable husband would be selected,

To become her husband and rule beside,

A man to comfort, rule and guide.

This was a question that would often rise,

In frustrated discussions and frustrated sighs,

As Elizabeth's council would try to convince,

That the queen couldn't rule without a good prince.

Try as they would, they couldn't persuade,
Their queen to marry, though plans were laid.
Though she kept them hopeful over the years,
Then hopes were dashed with frustrated tears.

Princes from foreign lands would arrive,
With plans of a marriage to contrive,
Hoping to get a positive reaction,
Aware of Elizabeth's political attraction.

But none succeeded, and would soon depart,
Though the queen often said they were her sweetheart.
She'd play the game and let them believe,
That they were the one, but just to deceive.

There was one man who people claimed,
Where her affections were clearly aimed.
A man who became more than a friend,
Or so gossip ran and their actions would lend.

Robert Dudley was the man she adored,
Childhood friends who struck that chord,
Within each other's heart and soul,
Who seemed to make each other whole.

Robert was married, but his wife was unwell,
And Elizabeth would often Robert tell,
That if he was free and his wife was dead,
Then together, in married bliss, they'd tread.

So, when Robert's wife died when she fell,
His enemies spoke and doubts would swell,
Drawing attention to their suspicion,
Of a man who was false and lacking contrition.

Yet, the coroner found her death accidental,
The time of her death coincidental.
But it gave Elizabeth her longed-for chance,
To pursue her yearning for romance.

The council reacted with words of advice,

Not mincing words and being precise,

Telling Elizabeth that if they were wed,

Rebellion, not joy, might follow instead.

Unlike her sister, who'd married regardless,

Whose political thoughts were blinkered and artless,

Elizabeth listened to what was advised,

The wisdom of councillors soon recognised.

Elizabeth knew that to become a bride,

Her control of the nation might gradually slide,

As she might be seen as a wife and no more,

Her husband supreme which she would abhor.

So, Elizabeth didn't marry her Robert,

Wasn't to love so blind a convert,

Remaining aloof and always chaste,

Remembering the lesson of marrying in haste.

But when Robert chose to marry again,

Elizabeth couldn't help to refrain,

From showing her outrage and displeasure,

To the woman who'd stolen her heart's single treasure.

Over the years, her advisers would learn,

That Elizabeth would all suitors spurn,

Keeping herself as a maid intact,

Making her councillors face the fact.

England and Scotland had often known tension,

Abiding so close in apprehension,

That the other was scheming to overthrow,

Their sovereign rights and lay them low.

Elizabeth inherited her nation's concern,

That Scotland's ambition might yet return,

To threaten the realm and Elizabeth's right,

To take her power to a greater height.

Scotland and France were a constant threat,
With a dangerous alliance which looked to be set,
To holding England in a terrible vice,
Which would make England pay the price.

So, Elizabeth sent a force to the north,
That France would be expelled henceforth,
Removing the threat in support of those,
Who similar protestant values chose.

Once a treaty with Scotland had been set,
And victorious forces in England were met,
Scottish pride was quickly regained,
When the Queen of Scotland was entertained.

Mary was linked to the Tudor line,
When her grandfather tried his house to align,
With Henry the Eighth through a marriage deal,
Which would, they hoped, a settlement seal.

Margaret Tudor was Mary's grandmother,
And Henry the Eighth was Margaret's brother.
So her claim to the English throne was sound,
A claim which would Elizabeth hound.

Mary had left her Scotland when five,
When only a child, and now would arrive,
As a queen which hardly anyone knew,
So, right from the start, suspicions grew.

Mary was catholic and followed its way,
While in Scotland the protestant cause held sway.
It was clear to the Scots that there would be a clash,
Should the queen their religious rights try to smash.

Concerned, Elizabeth would try to arrange,
A marriage for Mary so they could exchange,
A treaty whereby they'd be at peace,
That the tension between the nations might cease.

Robert Dudley at first was selected,

But this, by Queen Mary, was quickly rejected.

Then came Lord Darnley whose heritage was good,

From a family whose lineage was well understood.

Mary accepted, and soon they were married,

The queen, as a bride, over threshold carried,

But Darnley was not all that he seemed,

And hopes for the future were not redeemed.

When a son was born, people applauded,

As Scotland's prayers had been accorded,

With an heir that would at least ensure,

The reign of a king might be secure.

Yet, Darnley wasn't liked, and was murdered one night,

By Scottish Lords who soon hated his sight.

Fingers were pointed, and words were said,

That Lord Bothwell was the murderer's head.

Mary, by Bothwell, was then abducted,
To a place of his keeping then conducted,
Where, in time, the couple were joined,
As husband and wife, though rumours were coined.

Married to Bothwell, suspicions arose,
That Mary planned her husband's death throes,
With Mary's complicity in murder disputed,
Her rights to rule were no longer reputed.

She tried to fight the forces now stacking,
But Mary found that her cause was now lacking.
She was forced, by her lords, to abdicate,
Leaving her son in their hands to his fate.

Fleeing to England, Mary sought,
The love and support that she thought,
Her cousin to her cause would lend,
That Mary might her fortunes mend.

But Elizabeth listened to her council's plea,
That Mary should not be allowed to go free,
As she was a catholic queen to fear,
In a kingdom across the border so near.

So, Mary would live in a house of her own,
Where intrigues and plots were gradually sown.
Living in comfort, but closely observed,
The Queen of Scots life was harshly preserved.

For nineteen years, Mary would dwell,
In houses watched in a living hell.
Never free to go and come as she pleased,
The knowledge of imprisonment never eased.

Yet Mary's presence could only mean,
Her imprisoned status would be seen,
As the draw of rebels in the catholic cause,
Who'd topple Elizabeth and her protestant laws.

Rebels were crushed, but spies slipped through,
Catholic men who literally knew,
That if they were caught death awaited,
But their faith left many animated.

To help Elizabeth defeat all plots,
Which sought the rise of the Queen of Scots,
Sir Francis Walsingham was always there,
Breaking conspiracies and laying them bare.

Passionate for keeping her majesty protected,
He tortured suspects so plots were detected.
Men of intelligence were duly enrolled,
Forming a network which he controlled.

He hoped by his actions that the net would be closed,
Actions against the queen then exposed,
Revealing all plots as they were laid,
Arresting conspirators as they sought to evade.

One by one, he found and arrested,
Catholic plotters which he detested.
Tortured and punished for daring to tread,
On English soil, their treason to spread.

From humble beginnings, he would arise,
As Spymaster General with a network of spies.
Filled with a puritan protestant zeal,
With catholic supporters he was willing to deal.

Then one daring plot caught his attention,
Its plan and scope having great dimension,
Giving him proof that Mary was involved,
From which she couldn't be absolved.

This was what he'd sought to prove,
To show his queen she must remove,
Her cousin's head before she acted,
Before more traitors to her were attracted.

Sir Anthony Babington's coordination,
Of a plan for Elizabeth's termination,
Was devised to help catholic Mary assume,
England's throne by Elizabeth's doom.

Patient Walsingham let it mature,
Let plotters feel safe by success' allure,
Until, having proof, that all were committed,
Mary's guilt, to his queen, was duly submitted.

Letters were found proving her guilt,
So, a case against her was rapidly built.
Put on trial, Queen Mary was forced,
To hear the treason which she had endorsed.

But even then, the queen hesitated,
Unsure, uncertain and quite agitated.
While Walsingham wanted Mary's demise,
Elizabeth refused to give him his prize.

For she knew that Mary was of royal blood,
And taking her life would cause a flood,
Of foreign outrage and indignation,
And her death might be a martyr's creation.

At last, a warrant for death was signed,
Though Elizabeth's heart still felt inclined,
To act with caution lest Europe's perception,
Of what she'd done have a cold reception.

In fifteen eighty-seven, Mary was led,
To the block in Fotheringhay to lose her head.
She forgave the axeman, then prayed and knelt,
Until the deadly blows were dealt.

The reaction in Europe was as she suspected,
Her pleas of ignorance ignored and neglected.
Spain was indignant and promised to act,
And her words with power and wealth were backed.

Elizabeth hoped and always intended,
That England's trade should be extended,
Enabling her nation to grow and build,
When England's coffers were constantly filled.

Europe seemed the obvious choice,
For cunning traders to have a voice,
In all the business that was there,
Making a profit in deals that were fair.

English wool was in great demand,
And English merchants could command,
A price which would many enrich,
As businessmen made their selling pitch.

Being an island, men would explore,
Over the ocean to foreign shore,
Seeking new worlds where wealth might reside,
Their desire for treasure satisfied.

Far and wide the explorers would range,
Finding lands and peoples strange,
Hoping to fill their ships with gold,
Or precious things which could be sold.

Elizabeth knew that the key to survival,
Was having wealth which would at least rival,
The Spanish empire, which was her great threat,
And the cost of defence would have to be met.

So, Elizabeth welcomed all expeditions,
From men of vision and burning ambitions,
Who dared to cross the seas in their ships,
Men prepared to risk all on their trips.

Sir Francis Drake was one such as these,
Who sought great wealth and his queen to please,
By taking small ships across the great ocean,
Lurching and pitching with the seas mighty motion.

His voyages took him around all the earth,
In search of those things he thought might be worth,
Something for England and his queen back at home,
Leading him ever further to roam.

When his ship returned, Elizabeth boarded,
And there, on the deck, he was rewarded,
By a grateful queen, who would invite,
Drake to kneel and made him a knight.

But the Spanish saw Drake in a different way,
As a pirate whose actions they hoped to repay.
He hated the Spanish and attacked them at sea,
Fighting the Dons where e'er they might be.

For Spanish treasure ships were ripe,
With gold and silver to board and swipe,
To add to Elizabeth's coffers that swelled,
If England's safety were to be upheld.

And Elizabeth was even keenly prepared,
To send diplomats where few had yet dared,
Sending them out to travel far,
To eastern lands and the Russian Tsar.

From foreign shores the goods flowed in,
While England sold her wool and tin,
Also selling goods she produced,
As luxury items were introduced.

Distant lands were there to exploit,
For men who in business were adroit.
They gave the nation things yet unknown,
Where the seeds of a mercantile nation were sewn.

Yet England and Elizabeth were deceived,
If they ever really believed,
That affronts to Spain would go unchecked,
As indignant Spain sought all to correct.

Rivalry had grown between England and Spain,

Throughout Elizabeth's protestant reign,

To the point where Philip, the Spanish king,

Sought a conclusion at last to bring.

In the Netherlands, where the Spanish horde,

Had occupied lands and victories scored,

Elizabeth sent forces to relieve,

The protestant cause and hopes to retrieve.

At the Treaty of Nonsuch, Elizabeth vowed,

To aid Dutch rebels who refused to be cowed,

With troops being led by the Earl of Leicester,

But her lack of support, with him, would fester.

For Elizabeth's strategy was double edged,

Speaking words of peace, while support was pledged,

Leaving Leicester and his troops to make,

The best of their role for the protestant's sake.

A state of war was undeclared,

Though swords would clash as each prepared,

To deal the other a mortal blow,

The right of their cause to brutally show.

Spain had long since made the decision,

That both were now on war's collision,

And Philip of Spain had had too much,

Of England's piracy and helping the Dutch.

Treasure ships were attacked and plundered,

As guns in Spanish ports had thundered,

Now Philip's restraint for war had dried,

So, a different tactic would be applied.

When Mary Queen of Scots was slain,

No longer could King Philip constrain.

His desire to get his revenge at last,

To curb the English threat that was cast.

'The Enterprise of England', or so it was called,
Would leave the Catholic world enthralled,
Or so King Philip duly intended,
When so much Spanish wealth was expended.

A mighty Spanish fleet would depart,
And across the English Channel dart,
Taking a Spanish army across,
For England's punishment and her loss.

Intent on sailing and then to invade,
With a mighty force of ships arrayed,
The fleet set sail 'neath summer sky,
Confident that nothing could go awry.

They sailed through the channel to rendezvous,
With the Duke of Palma, whose forces drew,
Upon the Netherland's coast to meet,
This mighty Spanish invasion fleet.

As it sailed, it was intercepted,

By England's fleet which had been collected,

To counter the Spanish if it dared to mount,

Its plan to settle this old account.

But the Duke of Medina Sidonia was tasked,

With one single goal and Philip had asked,

That the Duke take the fleet to Palma who waited,

As this was the plan the king stipulated.

Thirty thousand troops were collected,

Whose skill in war had been perfected,

Waiting for the fleet to arrive,

That they could England of freedom deprive.

Medina Sidonia had been selected,

As a prominent noble who was highly respected.

Though he had his doubts about the campaign,

And courtiers blocked his attempt to complain.

The fleet then headed for the Dutch coast,
To pick up the army they needed most,
Intent on delivering sword and flame,
To put an end to England's game.

One hundred and thirty ships were amassed,
That England's people would be harassed,
When ships and men would be landed,
And Spain's dominions could be expanded.

On the south coast of England, beacons were lit,
When the Spanish were spotted, and so to transmit,
The signal that the foe was approaching,
In English waters were now encroaching.

Led by Lord Howard, the English set sail,
Hoping King Philip's plan to curtail.
Knowing that all their freedom depended,
On England's ships which freedom defended.

Yet Philip's zeal was filled with desire,
To throw English ambition upon the pyre,
Watching the threat to his empire fall,
That Spanish supremacy might yet stand tall.

So, the mighty armada off Calais appeared,
As no threat by England seemed volunteered,
Not worried the English might come and engage,
Oblivious to England's planned outrage.

Whilst Medina Sidonia and Palma strove,
To join their forces on foreign cove,
Drake let loose his plan at night,
To the Spaniard's alarm and panicked fright.

Drake had chosen several old craft,
Small, nimble and of shallow draught,
Which he promptly torched and set ablaze,
Which the Spanish saw with a panicked gaze.

The Spanish Armada was promptly scattered,

Its hopes of union with Palma shattered.

In the battle that followed, ships were damaged,

As English shot across them ravaged.

Then the wind began to suddenly shift,

And the Spanish fleet began to drift,

Moved by a sudden southwest wind,

Forcing the Spanish their plans to rescind.

As mighty sails filled with the breeze,

Wooden ships seemed to move with ease,

Their bows breaking water as each one ploughed,

Away from the cannons acrid cloud.

Battered and stunned, the Spanish withdrew,

With the English chasing as they flew.

Up England's east coast, the armada went,

Its zeal for invasion dwindled and spent.

Storms and tides took a great toll,

Leaving wrecks of great ships on rock and shoal.

Those who survived and didn't drown,

Were left to the mercies of each village and town.

As a woman, Elizabeth was supposed,

To consider marriage once a man proposed,

Then to do what her husband demanded,

To live in obedience and be commanded.

But Elizabeth was different, and was inclined,

Not to be ruled or be confined,

To obeying a man or being subdued,

Or at the whim of a husband's mood.

When young, she realised and took note,

Of how her world could be cutthroat,

With queens being ousted when the king had enough,

With politics treating women so rough.

Try as they might, men were unable,
To get her to marry, and so disable,
The image of Elizabeth ruling alone,
The sight of just a queen on the throne.

Suitors there were with loving intent,
Hoping a union with her to cement,
Yet Elizabeth wasn't really prepared,
To have her position as ruler shared.

In time, less pressure would be applied,
As courtiers saw she wouldn't be tried,
And fearing her wrath, less took the chance,
Though hoped she'd marry by circumstance.

Over the years, she courted the view,
Which time and experience would accrue,
Of a mystical figure which the nation beheld,
And in showing their love, most were compelled.

The queen knew the value of a positive appearance,

For the people to grow to willing adherence,

Of what she had planned, and where she would lead,

And the image of Elizabeth she'd happily feed.

Distinctive in her flamboyant dress,

Everyone recognised Good Queen Bess,

Displaying her power in grace and taste,

Her stature pronounced by the wealth interlaced.

Her dresses were not plain or cheap,

Costing her much to buy and upkeep.

With a bodice which was embroidered by hand,

With silk and gold thread making it grand.

The lace on her neck resembled a wing,

Tall and stiff, it appeared to swing,

As along the corridors Elizabeth glided,

The image of regal power provided.

Dresses were covered with allegory,

Pictures which told a secret story,

Imagery which her stance would project,

Things the viewer was free to detect.

In court, the courtiers sought the queen's favour,

That they might all her blessings savour,

Hoping, one day, to be suitably attired,

In wealth and glory which each required.

Called 'Gloriana' when the armada was broken,

Elizabeth was flattered by all the words spoken,

Which helped the image of her to deepen,

In the minds of her subjects she longed to sweeten.

Even as the queen grew older,

Courtiers hung about her shoulder,

Whispering words to beguile and flatter,

Trying to fool with flirting chatter.

Those at court would play and dance,
Hoping for that single chance,
To impress the queen and then to bask,
In favoured light, with favour to ask.

Yet Elizabeth played her courtiers too,
As every summer they wondered who,
Would have the pleasure of having her stay,
As her summer progress made its way.

For every year, the queen would depart,
From London's busy, noisy heart,
Taking her court to live and board,
At the house of a knight or well to do lord.

And all of her household would have to be fed,
As into the grounds her entourage spread.
From nobles to servants, each sought their spot,
Some getting nothing than a floor or a cot.

The queen enjoyed her music and dancing,
Pretending to flirt and be romancing,
With a young courtier on her arm,
Exuding skill, delight and charm.

Skill in the Galliard or Pavane's gentle strain,
Might help her courtiers to see and attain,
Memories of a queen who had been young,
Though the mark of time had already stung.

She played the virginal and the lute,
Achieving excellence of some repute,
Enjoying the pleasure she derived,
And the following praise that arrived.

Every year, the court would embark,
On a progress to houses that would mark,
A procession so people could testify,
To the joy of seeing their queen pass by.

As courtiers jostled for power and flattered,
Only their standing with Elizabeth mattered.
As she grew older, all those around,
Would speak of her youth and try to astound.

Words of praise appealed to her vanity,
Touching that part of Elizabeth's' humanity,
That craved affection from every person,
But knew the touch of age would worsen.

When Robert Devereaux, Earl of Essex,
Became the favourite of her subjects,
She gave him positions to keep him sweet,
Believing his love was pure and complete.

Men like these around her swarmed,
As factional politics were performed,
By men who were preoccupied,
Whose zeal for power was amplified.

Surrounded by men, ambitious and younger,

Men that for her favour would hunger,

Elizabeth felt a rejuvenation,

Youthful by association.

Yet, in many ways her image eroded,

As troubles on her realm unloaded.

The war with Spain hadn't yet ended,

While settlers in Ireland needs be defended.

Then poor harvests took a grip,

Causing the faith in the queen to dip.

Monopolies given raised many prices,

From basic goods to exotic spices.

The people started to feel a resentment,

Many losing their hope and contentment,

As Elizabeth's actions for troubles were blamed,

And saying her favoured men should be tamed.

The Earl of Essex was one who misused,
Elizabeth's favour, but was often excused,
As the queen, in him, could only see,
A faithful, youthful, loving trustee.

But Essex was pampered and had design,
For much more power for which he'd pine,
Leading him to raise a revolt,
Awaking the queen with a nasty jolt.

Yet the role of Essex, by most, was detested,
And soon it was over, and he was arrested.
Thrown into the tower to await a sentence,
Gone was his hubris and noble pretence.

His sentence of death could not be averted,
The call for justice not be perverted,
For Elizabeth knew he had to be flung,
To Death to appease each wagging tongue.

Life, it seemed, to Elizabeth contrived,
That fiends should die, while she survived.
With each new crushing fatality,
The queen saw her own mortality.

Every season must disappear,
Swept away by each passing year,
And try as she might to prolong and pretend,
Elizabeth's life to Death would descend.

Her life as a queen had had its effect,
Spent for the people she tried to protect.
Yet luxury also left its scar,
In the rise and fall of Elizabeth's star.

Underneath her wigs so red,
Was hair that was white, thinning and dead.
Her youthful looks hadn't quite fled,
With remaining beauty enhanced by lead.

Her love of sugar left teeth in decay,
Which, when she spoke, the gaps would betray.
Though she was weakened by years of duty,
Elizabeth tried to retain her beauty.

In sixteen O-three, the end would come,
A shock to many, a relief to some,
As most had wondered when it would finish,
When Elizabeth's reign would slow and diminish.

Her reign had been welcomed as a tonic,
A breath of fresh air that became iconic.
Though filled with trials and tribulation,
The nation remembers with fond admiration.

To more astute minds, the meaning was clearer,
As Elizabeth's death was the end of an era,
Which led the nation from the Middle Ages,
Opening up those Renaissance pages.

The Stuarts

Interesting Fact:

The name was originally spelled Stewart, and referred to The High Steward of Scotland, but Mary, Queen of Scots, was raised in France and she adopted the French way of spelling the name.

James I
(VI of Scotland)
(1603-1625)

Interesting Fact:

Though he was king of both England and Scotland, the English parliament refused to grant him the title of 'King of Great Britain' on legal grounds. However, James used the title anyway, although he was informed he could not use it on any documents which would be considered legal.

From fifteen sixty-seven James had been,
King of Scotland and showed he was keen,
To have the English throne as well,
In the richer court of England to dwell.

Though individual sovereign states,
James would shape both their fates,
By ruling each as their sovereign lord,
Though much resentment would be stored.

He believed that England and Scotland must,
Work together and build more trust,
With a single parliament for them both,
A single government taking the oath.

But nobles on either side of the border,
Preferred the old ways and the disorder,
Instead of two parliaments ruled by one man,
Spoke against change when talks began.

James also sought a peaceful path,
To avoid foreign war and its wrath,
When many nations became deeply involved,
In the Thirty Years War, that took time to resolve.

The English war with Spain would end,
As James spoke out and tried to defend,
His policy which was focused on peace,
Or the drain on his wealth would never cease.

Though England's religious attitude had,
Made life for the Catholics fairly bad,
But once the plot by Guy Fawkes failed,
Any thoughts of tolerance were curtailed.

But the gunpowder plot was soon uncovered,
The King and Parliament's fate recovered.
Just in time the plot had been spoiled,
And protestant fear of Catholics boiled.

While the Scottish kirk had left on him,
A strict belief, firm and grim,
Making James a religious terror,
Punishing Catholics he saw in error.

Such was the feeling and terrible fear,
That Catholics suffered should they adhere,
To their beliefs and then be caught,
Being hunted, it seemed, just for sport.

The fear of Catholics spread through the land,
And James was determined to take them in hand,
To try to put an end to their threat,
To catch as many as he could in his net.

Yet soon resistance would take shape,
To help the Catholic faith escape,
From all their pain and persecution,
Torture and then a quick execution.

So James continued to rule as he thought,
Regardless of what his actions brought.
Though King, he felt a constant suspicion,
That no one accepted his royal position.

He also wanted to build and expand,
A mighty empire by claiming land,
In Ireland and the Americas too,
Where colonies and ill feeling grew.

A scholar by nature, he preferred writing,
To the cost and ugly nature of fighting,
And if a solution could be found,
Better that choice than reason confound.

Like any monarch, he favoured those,
Who were handsome and wore all the right the clothes,
Of someone who was lively and bright,
A courtier he liked to keep in his sight.

Some were useful and helped him to take,
All those decisions he had to make,
Whilst others were there to entertain,
To love and cherish and share the strain.

The Duke of Buckingham was his best,
Who, with great favour, was constantly blessed,
And many a courtier was heard to say,
That James and the Duke lived happy and gay.

Yet, despite the gossip, and fingers pointed,
Ann, James's wife, did not feel disjointed,
From her husband and both of them smiled,
When she, twelve times, was expecting a child.

But the court was full of different factions,
Those jostling for power, position and actions,
Which might place them ever near,
To James and then to have his ear.

For James had shown that he was inept,
At dealing with government, so he kept,
His favourites in those council seats,
Whilst they gave him all manner of treats.

In no time at all, scandals evolved,
With several nobles deeply involved,
Which left the court of James very tainted,
With an image of corruption painted.

By early sixteen twenty-five,
James was barely still alive,
With illness and pressure of being king,
Etched on his face with the pain they could bring.

By March, the King was dying in bed,
After a stroke and dysentery led,
James to be taken to his own room,
And, with his favourite, lay in the gloom.

Charles I
(1625-1649)

Interesting Fact:

A very sickly child, Charles was left in Scotland whilst the rest of the family went to England. Only when he was three and a half and considered able to walk by himself for a short distance, was he allowed to join his family. However, his speech was slow to develop, and he always struggled with a stammer for the rest of his life.

In sixteen hundred, Charles was born,
But, at three, was rudely torn,
From his family when his father became,
The King of England to much acclaim.

Weak and sickly from his birth,
Few could see the prince's worth,
So Charles was kept back at home,
Until gaining the strength so he could roam.

At barely four, he was duly sent,
To England's court where he'd present,
Himself to England's nobility,
Greeted to smiles and civility.

Yet he couldn't quite shake his hesitant speech,
A stammer which family would beseech,
Young Charles to do his best to conceal,
As they thought it lacked a charm and appeal.

As the second son of the king and queen,
The face of Charles was rarely seen,
As all attention went to his brother,
Henry Frederick who the court would smother.

Charles thought his brother the perfect prince,
And didn't need courtiers to try and convince,
That Henry, as king, would be great,
But wicked and cruel was Henry's fate.

For when eighteen, Henry had died,
With the grief at court for James' pride,
For father, mother and brother too,
Lamented his loss, and their grief was true.

All of a sudden, their sickly child,
At twelve, would have to be schooled and styled,
As heir apparent with a new title,
His role in the dynasty now being vital.

When young, Prince Charles never supposed,
That the role of king would be proposed,
For he was the second son of James,
Never to hold those royal names.

In sixteen twenty-five, Charles was crowned,
And to the rule of England bound,
With people not knowing what this would entail,
Hoping that order and peace might prevail.

His father championed the protestant cause,
Dealing with Catholics without pause,
So, people hoped that Charles the first,
Would keep those feelings his father had nursed.

Long before his calling dawned,
His role as prince by James was pawned,
Hoping to gain alliance with Spain,
An act the people held in disdain.

King James thought Charles could be a match,
To the Spanish Infanta, and would be a catch,
But negotiations would fall apart,
As the Princess disliked him from the start.

The puritan part of England's belief,
Were filled with suspicion, fear and grief,
That James sought alliance through a Catholic bride,
A Protestant king who'd damaged their pride.

But in the end, he would marry,
A Bourbon princess who would carry,
Her Catholic faith to the throne,
Feeding suspicions and setting the tone.

Henrietta Maria of Catholic France,
Whom Charles would marry through fickle chance,
Would be seen as a thorn in his side,
In a Protestant England where she couldn't hide.

Having met Henrietta while he passed,
Through Paris when the spell was cast,
Charles felt sure there was a detection,
Of interest and some small affection.

When the deal with Spain had fallen through,
The course of Charles towards France blew.
Convinced of Henrietta's charm,
They wed by proxy at Notre Dame.

But protestant England would never trust,
Their king and Queen as people must,
And every time the king did wrong,
Thoughts of Catholic plots were long.

Like monarchs before, Charles believed,
The role of the King by God was conceived,
Thinking that what he did was right,
Regardless of anyone else's plight.

Yet England was home to those who were,
Filled with the zeal of the righteous and pure,
Of men and women who knew their god,
Would punish their king for not sparing the rod.

This was a time of religious zeal,
When the presence of God was near and real.
Protestant puritans who dearly craved,
To see God's face and then to be saved.

So, having a Catholic for their Queen,
Many believed it was a screen,
For catholic influence in the reign,
Which Charles had added to their pain.

With dreams of a protestant queen then crushed,
And then a marriage to a catholic rushed,
Some saw the new queen as an outsider,
A catholic and a protestant derider.

Yet the king was sure that God had set,

His plans in place that His will be met,

To make the nation a better place,

Which the people of England should accept and embrace.

Believing he only did God's will,

Charles would rule with little skill,

Making people begin to think,

That the monarch was leading them to the brink.

But despite professing God's affection,

His actions only caused objection,

As the court of Charles was seen as depraved,

Filled with those who to lusts were enslaved.

Charles had developed slowly when young,

Not swift of wit or nimble of tongue,

And despite the efforts to help with his grammar,

He always retained his hesitant stammer.

Those around him didn't care,
So long as Charles had favours to spare.
With words of advice to speak in his ear,
Hoping that Charles would keep them near.

The one who was the court's foremost,
Was the Duke of Buckingham, who was engrossed,
In keeping his place once James was dead,
Remaining the favourite and keeping ahead.

Yet, nothing would alter or distract,
The king of England from the fact,
That he believed God was his guide,
Always present and on his side.

But in March of sixteen twenty-eight,
Parliament was summoned to debate,
The right of the king to levy a tax,
Which Parliament thought a dangerous act.

Then Parliament's long Petition of Rights,
Set the House of Commons' sights,
On how the king should be contained,
And rights of Parliament were maintained.

This petition clearly displayed,
That Parliament would try to blockade,
Their king should he try to participate,
In acts he might try or anticipate.

And Charles and his queen soon fell out,
When he, due to faith, began to doubt,
That her Catholic practise caused no harm,
Giving him and his subjects some alarm.

Charles then broke the deal he agreed,
Sent troops to La Rochelle to make France Bleed,
In defence of the Huguenots who, Charles said,
Were Protestants fighting the catholic dread.

A tax without his Parliament's approving,
Caused Parliament's anger and its reproving.
Through due process, they tried to appeal,
Though Charles, to Parliament, wouldn't kneel.

In January sixteen twenty-nine,
Parliament, by Charles' grand design,
Was opened when he gave a speech,
Hoping the MP's minds to reach.

Tonnage and poundage was a tax introduced,
Centuries before that wealth be produced,
From goods that were daily imported,
But the tax, over years, had become distorted.

Some felt the imposition of these dues,
Was against the Petition of Rights and views,
Which said that Parliament should hold power,
Not be the king's puppet and simply cower.

Charles then called for the House to adjourn,
But MP's knew the king wouldn't learn,
Unless they acted and showed what they felt,
So they had to move fast that the lesson be dealt.

The acts were read out, and well received,
As those in the House mostly believed,
That Charles would have to do as they bid,
Not thinking that Charles would do as he did.

For the king was angry, and retaliated,
In a way which simply illustrated,
His belief in his right to do as he felt,
Regardless of consequence, or what actions spelt.

Charles simply had his Parliament dissolved,
Believing his problems would be resolved.
To also show that he must be obeyed,
Nine members of Parliament were arrested and paid.

Royalist sympathies were still quite strong,
Believing that power should still belong,
To the king whatever problems arose,
Following along each path he chose.

Yet the king had clearly demonstrated,
His ruling should be moderated,
By others who might have the vision,
To see each problem and division.

Despite his heavy hand approach,
The fear of debt would still encroach,
Leaving his plans badly tattered,
Hopes of successful leadership scattered.

Facing debt, Charles had no choice,
But to seek his Parliament's voice,
In giving assent on granting him cash,
Exposed to their words and a firm backlash.

Although the king could always count,
On the House of Lords who'd always mount,
A keen defence for his royal person,
Hoping his status wouldn't worsen.

Yet there were those in the House of Lords,
Who saw the problem and leaned towards,
The House of Commons and what they stood for,
And the fears of the people which they bore.

Whatever laws and Acts were passed,
Whatever accusations were cast,
The Lords would have to soon decide,
To challenge their king, or his ways abide.

In March sixteen forty, Parliament convened,
With true intentions carefully screened,
Longing to work to their objective,
Not just to Charles' own directive.

For Parliament had only been recalled,
When Charles' war with the Scots was stalled,
Only wanting to use all the MP's
Believing they'd grant his desire with ease.

Yet Parliament hadn't forgotten a thing,
Clearly aggrieved and remembering,
All the trouble they'd had in the past,
Thinking they had the king at last.

The house agreed to grant revenue,
Giving respect to the king that was due,
If the 'ship money' tax was amended,
If the hated tax was finally ended.

Charles was having to face their nerve,
Demands from which they wouldn't swerve.
Clearly, they hadn't their grievance forgotten,
Their firm defiance having stronger gotten.

In March, there was a general election,
Which caused the king much sad reflection,
As candidates of Charles lost their seats,
Causing much gossip on London's streets.

For Parliament wanted more concessions,
Were daring with their loud expressions,
Trying to make the king concede,
To see, at last, the nation's need.

Two of Charles' friends pursued,
To broker a deal they thought was shrewd.
The Earls of Northumberland and Strafford failed,
To get the king money when plans were unveiled.

They said the king might soon relent,
On 'ship money' tax if cash was sent,
To his court for his Scottish attack,
To keep the king's offensive on track.

Yet Parliament could not give it's backing,
As a general consensus was found to be lacking.
The House was filled with a loud commotion,
With the wrath of Charles being set in motion.

Having the House of Lords support,
Charles felt his case could still be fought,
So Parliament, again, was duly dismissed,
Causing outrage in his Parliament's midst.

For less than a month, the MP's had sat,
Their hopes for reform soon falling flat,
As Charles, yet again, showed them all,
Parliament was there for his beck and call.

November, sixteen forty, England would see,
Parliament assemble to debate and agree,
On how they could work to at last prevent,
Disbandment of Parliament with the king's assent.

Elections were held, and the king's supporters,
Lost seats in the House in many quarters.
Much royal propaganda was heard and spun,
With just one hundred and forty-three seats won.

Three hundred and fifty seats were held,
By Parliamentarians, whose numbers swelled.
Most to the king weren't well disposed,
And, almost at once, change was proposed.

MP's power seemed to know no bounds,
As the House would echo to voice and sounds,
Of a Parliament which with life was filled,
As its breath of life into England spilled.

Soon the Commons would have to debate,
England's condition and Parliament's fate.
But previous sessions only indicated,
How Charles had bullied and dictated.

Now MP's would try to find a solution,
To bolster this ancient institution,
By giving it power not to be shunned,
Leaving the king and his courtiers stunned.

In sixteen forty-one, they gained a new lease,
Whereby it's influence might start to increase,
Giving MP's a much better chance,
To have more say, and it's say to enhance.

With the Triennial Act that was passed,
Every three years the House would be asked,
To come together and explore,
Matters which Charles could not ignore.

No longer needing the king's approval,
Charles couldn't order their sudden removal.
A grasp at power by the Commons was meant,
And Charles was obliged to give his consent.

It was October, sixteen forty-one,
And just as the killing had begun,
The old English in Ireland threw in their lot,
With the Gaelic Irish whose vengeance ran hot.

In the Commons, the rebels were seen,
As Catholic traitors whose acts were obscene.
Protestant settlers were brutally slain,
Subjected to torture, outrage and pain.

Yet Charles was seen as slow and inept,
As the wave of fear over England swept.
He asked the Commons for funds to raise,
An army to end those rebellious ways.

But Parliament suspected and perceived,
That they, by Charles, might be deceived,
Believing he might then use that strength,
To reverse all setbacks he'd suffered at length.

An army was needed to quickly deal,
With the Irish threat, which was very real,
As Protestants for the fight were braced,
Believing that Catholic intrigue was faced.

By the end of the year, in November,
Parliament showed its mood and temper,
By taking a more belligerent stance,
Composing for Charles their Grand Remonstrance.

But the document held more in store,
Attacking the king's reign at its core,
By demanding Bishops should be expelled,
With official appointments reduced, not swelled.

It also stated that Charles must show,
His acceptance that Parliament could always veto,
Anyone the king might choose to appoint,
To be an official and with power anoint.

With the document out and disclosed,
The King's delay was quickly exposed.
But when, at last, he deemed to reply,
Most of the points he would seek to deny.

In January, sixteen forty-two,
Tension in the nation grew,
As the struggle for power intensified,
With greater hostility identified.

For Charles took steps that were too drastic,
Desperate, severe and so fantastic,
That those in the Commons were agitated,
And anger with Charles was cultivated.

Then a critical point was reached,
With rumours Parliament would impeach,
The Queen, who was said to be conspiring,
With Irish rebels and their cause inspiring.

Charles then sent his troops to arrest,
Five of the House who'd done their best,
To try to steal his powers away,
Members of Parliament who'd had their say.

But word of the action reached them all,
Allowing the House to thwart and forestall,
An act which was seen as so aggressive,
And not, as Charles hoped, as impressive.

In typical fashion, Charles had reacted,
With the issue getting more protracted,
And when the Tower of London was placed,
In his control it caused distaste.

Each, to the other, was a constant thorn,
Full of rhetoric and of scorn.
For years suspicion had been fed,
And only war could lie ahead.

Men on both sides would fight and revere,
The cause of dull Roundhead or bright Cavalier.
Men took up arms to fight a crusade,
For a different England to be made.

By the summer, both sides were arming,
With levels of distrust alarming.
Parliament saw Charles as arrogant, deceptive,
While he saw Parliament as unreceptive.

With more negotiations rapidly failing,
And a mood of aggression now prevailing,
In August Charles decided to raise,
His standard and set the nation ablaze.

What followed were years of war and destruction,
As King and Parliament sought the other's destruction,
But in the end, Parliament had won,
Their King's attempts at supremacy done.

And Parliament showed what it truly felt,

When in sixteen forty-nine it dealt,

A punishment for their King's brutal acts,

Delivering him to the executioner's axe.

The Commonwealth

Interesting Fact:

During its eleven-year existence, no government of any real stability could be formed, and none lasted more than a few months. Though many different variations were tried, and parliaments were called, it was only the personality and force of Cromwell who kept the whole fragile system together.

Oliver Cromwell (Lord Protector) (1653-1658)

Interesting Fact:

One of ten children, Oliver was the only boy to survive into adulthood. Later, he was so disillusioned with how things were in England, that he tried to emigrate to the American colony of Connecticut but was not given permission to leave.

In April of fifteen ninety-nine,
When Tudor power was in decline,
He entered a world that wholly embraced,
Religious beliefs which life interlaced.

Born at the end of the Tudor reign,
To a Huntingdon family that was rather plain,
Modest gentry who could clearly trace,
Their line to Cromwell who served the Kings grace.

As a young man, he'd worship and praise,
God above in definite ways,
Showing a faith that was simple and pure,
A belief in God that would endure.

Then, in his thirties, he underwent,
A deeply personal, spiritual event,
When he had a religious conversion,
Leading him to a puritan immersion.

By sixteen twenty, he'd gained a wife,
Elizabeth Bourchier, to share his life,
And over the years, nine children were born,
Three dying young and from them torn.

Yet Oliver had a time of despair,
Doubts and depression, he couldn't bear,
A personal crisis which he weathered,
His faith in religion temporarily severed.

In time, with help, a new faith sprung,
Deep, powerful and always young,
With which he'd use to justify,
His path in life and battle cry.

Then fate delivered one more thing,
Which would to Oliver fortune bring,
With an uncle's property in Ely inherited,
Which Oliver thought by God was merited.

By sixteen forty, King Charles had ruled,
For years by himself, but the fire hadn't cooled,
As militant puritans hadn't forgotten,
All their king's faults they saw as rotten.

As MP for Cambridge, Oliver headed,
From Ely to London where was embedded,
All the intrigue of political suspense,
Where the great divide would soon commence.

Sitting alongside his puritan brothers,
Some saying he owed his position to others,
Oliver tried to ignore the rumour,
That he owed his seat to some gentleman's humour.

But when war with the king was finally entered,
Oliver, for the Parliament, ventured,
To show his belief for reform was sincere,
And that his commitment would never veer.

Throughout the war, he steadily rose,
Despite all hardship, highs and lows,
Showing his skill in all warfare,
In which few of the time could compare.

With the New Model Army for him to lead,
The soldiers of England became a new breed,
Of troops who were feared and respected,
Their skill at arms slowly perfected.

Then, at Preston, with the army he led,
The Royalist force was cut to a shred,
By the tactics and skill Oliver used,
Which left the enemy bloodied and bruised.

He believed his success was clearly sent,
From heaven above and God's intent,
In using key men to bring about,
A land which was worthy and devout.

When Charles was tried and sentenced to die,
Some of his foes would talk and try,
To find a way out of signing the warrant,
That would see his blood flow in a torrent.

Yet Oliver was the third who signed,
Which their king to death assigned.
Reluctant men were forced to decide,
Signing the warrant for regicide.

Once Charles was beheaded, a new state was declared,
A republic in which the people shared,
Or so they believed once the fighting stopped,
Once the power of kings was finally cropped.

A 'Commonwealth of England' with Parliament's rump,
The body of power cut to a stump,
That would, they thought, be a blessing,
With all the grievances soon addressing.

Oliver, with others, had been appointed,
To a council of state as England's anointed,
Guiding the nation for the common good,
With hopes for a common brotherhood.

Oliver's days of war weren't to end,
When the new regime decided to send,
Him and the army across the sea,
To Ireland to force parliamentary decree.

In sixteen fifty-three, he demanded,
The Rump disband and then be handed,
To a caretaker power that was a construction,
Of MP's and army who might suffer instruction.

Consisting of just forty seats,
Oliver hoped there'd be no repeats,
Of debates and Bills which only ignored,
The England he hoped to move toward.

But the Rump returned to its own debating,
Its own prestige and power inflating,
So Oliver changed the situation,
Much to parliament's protestation.

With forty troops he entered the hall,
Intent on seeing that parliament fall.
Taking parliament's ceremonial mace,
He sent MP's away in disgrace.

A new assembly was to be compiled,
Who, as saints, were to be styled,
Men whose faith was pure and intense,
Who didn't show any false pretence.

But this zealous Parliament of the Saints,
Was feared too righteous and had its taints,
As radical men had the majority,
And might abuse their new authority.

This Barebones Parliament eventually voted,
That its own dissolution should be promoted.
For just a few months, MP's attended,
The parliament until it was suspended.

Then shortly after its dissolution,
They found a speedy substitution,
When John Lambert, a general, had suggested,
That power, in one, should be invested.

Oliver Cromwell was the man he named,
Pious, brave and for battle famed,
And in December it was decreed,
That as Lord Protector he should proceed.

Yet his faith was never sacrificed,
As daily he sought the wisdom of Christ,
To help him rule as he felt he should,
To lead in the way he felt God would.

Under him, a parliament was shaped,
Men whose piety around them draped,
To debate on how to build and repair,
And how to end the people's despair.

Parliament could, under him, be dissolved,
A new one formed when he felt resolved.
But he had to go through a council of state,
To get a majority to decide England's fate.

But Oliver, also, was just a person,
And temptation for power would only worsen,
With men giving honour to England's trustee,
Given wealth and signing as Oliver 'P'.

In time, he'd be offered the crown to wear,
King Oliver the First for all to declare.
Though offered, Oliver flatly refused,
Having seen the role of king so abused.

In sixteen fifty-five, Royalists rebelled,
Hoping their rebellion spelled,
The end of the republic and the recall,
Of the monarchy that seemed to enthral.

But the planned rebellion wasn't supported,
Recruits for the Royalists couldn't be courted,
So the few who rose up were soon overcome,
Aware they'd have to flee or succumb.

Yet the Lord Protector still maintained,
Puritan souls should be restrained,
And not to react or be frightened,
But to walk with God and be enlightened.

To this end, he planned to invite,
The Jews back to England that they might,
Bring wealth and no longer be the pariah,
And might herald the coming of the messiah.

In sixteen fifty-seven, during his ruling,
After months of effort that were gruelling,
The offer of king had arisen,
But Oliver wouldn't to reason listen.

He chose to remain as Protector instead,
To leave the rank of king as dead,
Believing in God's intent and salvation,
That God had determined to end that vocation.

At Westminster Hall, on King Edward's chair,
Oliver Cromwell would promise and swear,
To follow the Humble Petition and Advice,
A constitution he could not sacrifice.

Under his direction, the nation earned,
Greater respect and a corner was turned,
As foreign powers were forced to concur,
That respect on England they must confer.

But like all men, the Protector was mortal,
Who longed to pass through the heavenly portal.
A man who had lived and was then getting old,
Who longed to see God and his face to behold.

In sixteen fifty-eight, the Protector grew weak,
In pain, he found it harder to speak,
And in September, after an illness,
His mind and body at last knew stillness.

Oliver Cromwell at last found peace,
Ending the burden and finding release.
He believed he knew where he belonged,
Wishing it wouldn't be prolonged.

Some would regret Oliver dying,
The man they believed was edifying,
Whilst many were happy and were elated,
Having heard of the death of him they hated.

Whatever the feeling, they had to accept,
That as a leader he wasn't inept.
In time, some critics would try to poor blame,
On the work he did and extinguish his flame.

Oliver Cromwell never sought the road,
To power or glory but had it bestowed,
By fate through unfortunate circumstance,
Perhaps by God or by fickle chance.

The mantle of power soon was passed,
To Richard, his son, but couldn't last,
As Richard's power base was slim,
With the prospect of success looking dim.

But he tried to go on as his father had wished,
Yet the strength of his father was sorely missed,
Leaving the new protector adrift,
Not having his father's leadership gift.

For eight long months Richard struggled,
As he led the nation and power juggled,
Doing his best to emulate,
His father's skill to arbitrate.

It seemed like the role of protector was spent,
As various factions seemed free to vent,
Thoughts of the future and their concern,
That perhaps to the past they might return.

By May of sixteen fifty-nine,
Richard's hold was in decline,
With calls for a king rapidly growing,
The wind of change steadily blowing.

The role which Richard Cromwell held,
Meant the Protector was compelled,
To face the truth, and was inclined,
To walk away and so resigned.

The Restoration

Interesting Fact:

Not everyone wanted the monarchy to return, and General John Lambert, one of parliament's top soldiers, tried to form an army of opposition but many deserted him, and he was eventually captured by Colonel Richard Ingoldsby, who had sat as a judge in the trial of Charles I and signed the King's death warrant.

Charles II
(1660-1685)

Interesting Fact:

The court of Charles II was considered by his protestant subjects to be lewd and immoral, and this view only grew worse when their king had many mistresses and eventually fathered at least a dozen illegitimate children.

In exile, the King made a proclamation,
Much to the people's acclamation,
In which he promised a national pardon,
If to the Republic they all would harden.

Most in the land would soon be driven,
By knowledge that they would be forgiven,
By Charles if everyone saw and accepted,
Republic beliefs must be rejected.

General Monck, a roundhead official,
Saw this deal could be beneficial,
So had a parliament quickly arranged,
That the form of government could be exchanged.

Monck had the army at his back,
A power base no-one could crack.
His march to London was unopposed,
With plans for change soon exposed.

A parliament was formed that, it said,
Didn't owe allegiance but, instead,
Was a parliament that talked at liberty,
To clear Charles' path to victory.

Filled with Royalist sympathisers,
And the republic's critisisers,
It met to vote for the restoration,
Of Kings and republic's ruination.

In an age when people felt suspicion,
With anything breaking the old tradition,
Republican values only appeared,
To destroy the values they revered.

On the eighth of May, sixteen sixty,
Members of Parliament would agree,
To vote on Charles the Second's reign,
Which would the gap of years explain.

They agreed to choose an important date,
Which would in people's minds create,
Thoughts that the strange republican age,
Hadn't existed on the political stage.

So, Charles was then officially declared,
To have ruled when regicide was dared,
His reign beginning with his father's demise,
The years in between lost in disguise.

Charles the Second returned to the land,
To a welcome which was seen as grand,
As many believed that divine order,
Would be restored within England's border.

After having spent nine long years,
In exile abroad with many fears,
The day came at last when he would be,
Crowned as king and from exile set free.

His return was marked with much celebration,
People rejoicing without hesitation,
As many people had in time felt,
Cromwell's rule had misery dealt.

A Royalist parliament was compiled,
By the king who once was poor and exiled.
For seventeen years this parliament remained,
By the grace of God and their king ordained.

Soon the king would turn his fury,
To the men who made the court and jury,
Which sent his father to the grave,
And to many his retribution gave.

Even the dead were not to be spared,
As each, in turn, were traitors declared.
Cromwell's body was then exhumed,
As the rage of revenge in England loomed.

Charles was young, flamboyant, tall,
And, in time, would show them all,
How a king should run his court,
With pleasure and distraction sought.

Yet, Charles was a king who also knew,
Not to give power to a dangerous few,
Showing more interest in understanding,
His government's work, which was quite demanding.

His conscience told him to tolerate,
The English Catholics, though some couldn't wait,
To create several laws which would persecute,
Catholics whose place was becoming acute.

He then had to face a war with the Dutch,
With his role as leader not leading to much,
But Charles was forced to ask for aid,
From the French king with promises made.

Under this treaty, Charles had agreed,
To Catholic conversion one day to concede,
Though he kept it a secret as long as he could,
As this, to the people, was not very good.

Like other Kings, Charles took a wife,
Catherine of Braganza, who, in her life,
Wasn't able to give him an heir,
Though by mistresses he had plenty to spare.

Charles loved the ladies and they swarmed,
For favour or love which left his bed warmed,
Giving him sons and daughters who,
Were given titles, some of them new.

Under his rule, people were feeling,
Free once more, with life more appealing,
With shows on stage far more relaxed,
As bawdy actors more eloquently waxed.

This merry monarch was for fun and cheer,
Colourful, happy and would steer,
The people's idea of how to behave,
Allowed the pursuit of what they would crave.

Though Charles wasn't just about fun and vice,
As fun and leisure would not suffice,
To satisfy Charles's burning desire,
To learn more things, from which he'd not tire.

For this was a great scientific age,
And his love of knowledge would set the stage,
For the great men to pursue their field,
Of scientific research, and what it would yield.

Men like Newton, Clarke, Neile and Hook,
Helped the King study and look,
At the world in a different light,
Giving him wonder and a great insight.

Then, in sixteen sixty-two,
Charles gladly assisted in something new,
By granting a coveted royal charter,
Which was the Royal Society's starter.

A Royal Observatory was also founded,
At Greenwich that France's lead be confounded,
In being the first to discover and name,
Planets and stars with their subsequent fame.

Yet, after just a few years had passed by,
The nation was racked by the mournful cry,
Of people whose loved ones had been stricken,
By plague which made them quickly sicken.

In the summer of sixteen sixty-five,
When the rats and fleas could easily thrive,
The numbers of dead from the plague rose,
The living left watching the dying death throes.

By July, the King had chosen to leave,
Leaving the rest of the city to grieve,
Where a quarter of those left in the city,
Died from the plague, many left without pity.

Then in sixteen sixty-six a fire,
Broke out in the city and things looked dire,
As the flames engulfed and rapidly spread,
Through the centre, filling people with dread.

Four long days and nights it raged,
Its appetite seemingly unassuaged,
As the old buildings with old wooden frames,
Were soon ignited and went up in flames.

But once the strong east wind had dropped,
The advance of the fire was mostly stopped,
Helped by explosives to make some breaks,
Though the threat remained from embers and flakes.

The fire, though bad, had cleared the way,
For the king and architects to have their say,
On how a new London should be reborn,
Once the old heart from the city was torn.

From it would come more stone than wood,
Buildings which have 'til this day stood,
With elegant fronts, ornate and tall,
With St. Paul's cathedral the best of them all.

But Charles was facing increasing stress,
From the line of succession, which was a mess,
As without a legitimate son to follow,
To some the alternative looked fairly hollow.

For James, his brother, was next in line,
But he was a Catholic, to some a sign,
That he'd return England to the old ways,
Where England gave Rome its wealth and praise.

A move against James was introduced,
Into Parliament and soon produced,
Those who supported it and those who opposed,
So, Charles took action, and had parliament closed.

What followed was by many described,
As tyranny with opposition proscribed,
As the rule of Charles became absolute,
His hold on power more resolute.

Though his absolute rule would not last,
For the health of the king was failing fast,
And upon his deathbed he was received,
Into the faith in which James believed.

James II
(1685-1688)

Interesting Fact:

When only three years old, James was made Lord High Admiral, a mainly honorary position within the Royal Navy. Then, at just nine years old, he was made a colonel in charge of an infantry regiment during the civil war.

The second son of Charles the First,
Just like his father he also nursed,
A desire to show who was in charge,
And royal powers to enlarge.

His Catholic faith was tolerated,
Though many despised and even hated,
The thought of their king being tied,
To the Pope, and Rome being his guide.

But tolerance of him did not extend,
To private people, who'd have to mend,
Their beliefs or then be chastised,
For the religion which many despised.

Almost at once, rebellion occurred,
As even the King's nephew preferred,
A monarch who wasn't attached or believed,
In Catholic ways, which most said just deceived.

Lyme Regis in Dorset is where it began,
The Duke of Monmouth being the man,
Who challenged his uncle's sacred right,
To rule as king and so offered the fight.

Monmouth had tried to coordinate,
With forces in Scotland but they met their fate,
When the forces of James quickly succeeded,
In facing the rebels when they were needed.

It was left to Monmouth, to raise the force,
That would march upon that course,
Of rebellion with hopes they could remove,
James from his throne and their cause prove.

At the Battle of Sedgemoor, the armies met,
Though the Duke had tried but failed to get,
Much support and was defeated with ease,
And the Duke's execution would James appease.

Throughout the west country, judges were sent,
Their fierce punishments clearly meant,
To show how James to rebels reacted,
Judge Jeffreys in Dorset being very distracted.

James did his best to have parliament change,
Laws against Catholics which he felt strange,
But parliament would not listen or see,
So, James tried to change the laws by decree.

Once more it was king against all of those,
Sitting in Parliament which people chose,
To help with ruling instead of just,
One man whose rule should be discussed.

When James had a son, most people knew,
That as he was taught and the boy grew,
James would see to making sure,
The Catholic faith would have its allure.

Parliament feared there would be a return,
To a Catholic dynasty and a spurn,
Of protestant ways which only bred,
A sense of worry, contempt and dread.

Many also had a deep suspicion,
That James had given himself a mission,
With his daughter excluded from the succession,
With his Catholic son set for his accession.

For his daughter, Mary, had married a prince,
William, a protestant, who need not convince,
The English parliament that he would be fit,
To rule their nation should fate permit.

By June of sixteen eighty-eight,
English nobles decided the fate,
Of England and James by what they proposed,
That William be king with James deposed.

William accepted and plans were made,
For his large army to invade,
An army filled with veterans who,
Were disciplined and their trade they knew.

In November, William's army arrived,
But James's force was soon deprived,
Of generals and men as many defected,
Their lack of faith in James not detected.

James had fought well in France years ago,
Was a brave soldier but now didn't know,
What he should do and chose not to engage,
Threw away the great seal in a fit of rage.

Soon king James was a prisoner in,
The Tower of London with no hope to win,
But William decided to let him escape,
As death would allow a martyr to shape.

James quickly fled to the French Court,
Where protection and resources were sought,
To give to James the chance to attain,
His kingdom or the fight to sustain.

By now, William and parliament met,
Discussed the issues and plans were set,
By which many saw the only solution,
Was seeing this as their Glorious Revolution.

But James wasn't finished and with French aid,
An attempt by him was quickly made,
When he landed in Ireland, where he received,
Support from those who in James believed.

William's response was, as predicted,
Quick, efficient and with James depicted,
As the Catholic threat which needed destroying,
A threat the new order found very annoying.

So, to Ireland, William sailed,

And there, at the Boyne, his army prevailed,

With James, once more, abandoning all,

Leaving his chances, and army, to fall.

William III (1689-1702) & Mary II (1689-1694)

Interesting Fact:

Although invited to rule England by the English parliament, William found himself at war with France in the Nine Years War, leaving Mary to do most of the ruling.

This Prince of Orange soon became,
Better known by another name,
As William the Third, and with his wife,
Lived a sound protestant life.

Mary, the daughter of Charles the First,
Was, in royal ways rehearsed,
Which left the people in little doubt,
Of what their noble queen was about.

Their protestant ways were seen by most,
As strict and true so many would boast,
That William, the soldier of God, provided,
Skills that could to war be guided.

For he was seen as the man to lead,
The fight against Catholics, to make them bleed,
As part of the ongoing wars which had,
Left nations in Europe feeling so bad.

But many in England refused to accept,
The wave of acceptance which had swept,
Throughout the land and which proclaimed,
A new King and Queen had been named.

Some still believed in that divine right,
Bestowed by God and yet despite,
Knowing they couldn't say too much,
To hopes of rebellion, they'd dearly clutch.

With his Dutch generals, William succeeded,
In defeating those rebels who victory needed.
Irish and Scottish rebels were forced,
To negotiate, with the new rule endorsed.

Though in Scotland William's reputation,
Suffered a severe deflation,
When, at Glencoe, killings occurred,
When rebels, unsure, a delay preferred.

A deadline for rebels to come in and surrender,
Missed by those who thought William the pretender,
Was dealt with by a violent reaction,
With William forced to punish the faction.

In Parliament, he favoured a balanced stance,
Not wishing to give any faction the chance,
Of controlling the House, then to dictate,
Their Policy and then his plans to frustrate.

Whigs and Tories were factions that,
Together in Parliament debated and sat,
Doing their best to ruin the schemes,
Like two opposing, belligerent teams.

Yet both, in time, would gain his attention,
As each, with the King, found dissension,
Which led the King to give and then switch,
Favour with one, and the other one ditch.

More war with France didn't help things,
With two very determined religious Kings,
But William needed to gain the approval,
Of MP's and couldn't just seek their removal.

To help with funds, a new bank was created,
A bank of England which Whigs advocated,
To give to King and England more,
A bank set up in sixteen ninety-four.

But as the war with France progressed,
William, more and more was pressed,
To be away from the English throne,
Leaving Mary to try and rule alone.

Yet Mary could only act on advice,
Given by William, which was precise,
With William ruling through his Queen,
With William's touch through her seen.

Nine years of war with France had led,
To high taxation and people said,
That trade and business would be affected,
If the cares of the people were neglected.

In sixteen ninety-four, the king was shaken,
When Mary, by smallpox, was quickly taken,
Leaving him to rule on his own,
Which caused lots of people to sadly bemoan.

Three years later, war with France ended,
Words of peace and friendship pretended,
With France clearly stating it would not give,
More aid to rebels that rebellion might live.

Former King James would have to find,
Assistance and aid of another kind,
Which left his cause almost broken,
Though defiant words by him were spoken.

With further bloodshed having been averted,
The French King to William's rights converted,
Both countries could at last get back,
To getting their economies on the right track.

Then there arose an awkward question,
Which dealt with the Spanish King's succession.
Talks were held, France and England agreed,
As to what would happen and who'd succeed.

But the dying king of Spain nominated,
A Frenchman and so all hope was deflated,
As he was the French King's own grandson,
So, France claimed the throne, and peace was done.

July of seventeen 0-one then saw,
A conflict which struck at Europe's core,
A war which would last longer than thought,
One of the longest the nations had fought.

In the same year as the war commenced,
William's thoughts on succession sensed,
That his lack of children could only mean,
Steps must be taken for this trouble foreseen.

But the Act of Succession was duly passed,
That James's exclusion might continue to last,
Thereby denying him and his line,
From retaking the throne by any design.

Mary's sister, Anne, would follow,
By an Act to leave all other claims hollow,
And if she had no heirs, the throne would pass over,
To a distant relative in the House of Hanover.

It was well that William had this resolved,
As his personal situation evolved,
For by the March of seventeen 0-two,
Death by pneumonia meant his reign was through.

Anne
(1702-1714)

Interesting Fact:

Anne, and her sister Mary, were the only two of eight children to survive into adulthood. Anne herself was pregnant seventeen times, but not one child survived, which deeply affected her.

The daughter of James the Second, who,
Was deposed as fears from religion grew,
Nobody could have dreamt or supposed,
She'd one day be Queen, after he was deposed.

Once her sister and William were invited,
To claim the throne hopes were ignited,
That Anne, one day, might realise,
The role of Queen, the ultimate prize.

In seventeen 0-two, Anne was prepared,
To take the crown and so was declared,
Queen of England with hopes that she,
Might be a balance between Whig and Tory.

But the Tories were the ones she favoured,
Who for moderation laboured,
Unlike the Whigs whose ways she felt,
Were radical and more trouble spelt.

Anne had inherited a war to direct,
Or else let the plans of France go unchecked,
With the War of the Spanish Succession raging,
Both nations in brutal battles engaging.

Yet Anne had a friend who was always there,
To help her with any stress or care,
Sarah Churchill, who was always nearby,
To listen, advise or act as a spy.

Whatever went on in the English court,
Sarah's opinion or favour was sought,
For she was the favourite, Anne's very best friend,
And if Anne had a problem, for Sarah she'd send.

In time, it was Sarah that courtiers sought,
To gain her favour and support,
Knowing that she had the Queen's trust,
That Sarah's word could make or bust.

Sarah's husband, John Churchill, was away,
Fighting the war and would display,
A skill for leadership and had attained,
Success and fame which he had maintained.

And whilst foreign armies by John were fought,
England's trade to the world was brought.
Through winning wars and spreading trade,
English strength and wealth were laid.

As England's prowess onwards trekked,
Some other realms were nearly wrecked.
For decades, France had always chosen,
War and strife where trade was frozen.

So, England's mighty war machine,
Was now skilled, well led and keen.
Once more it turned those foreign flanks,
Turned them with those blood red ranks.

From now on, this land would teach,
That it loved to trade, loved free speech.
Foes would learn as their plans were tossed,
That England's heart wasn't made of frost.

Anne depended on Sarah so much,
Because Sarah added her special touch,
To a life which had seen its fair share,
Of love, tragedy and a mother's despair.

Married to George, Prince of Denmark,
This royal couple would embark,
On producing seventeen children in all,
Yet all seventeen to death would fall.

With the loss of her children, one by one,
Sarah's web of support was soon spun,
Where Anne found comfort in having her near,
Her greater dependency being clear.

Then came a new and strange situation,
Which saw the birth of a brand-new nation,
When England and Scotland joined as one,
Their age-old division finally done.

It came when finances were hit hard,
When Europe's leaders were on their guard,
As each faced the task of making ends meet,
And for Scotland poverty was almost complete.

Then came a scheme which gave many hope,
The Darien Scheme of such scope,
It promised to give economies health,
So, Scotland invested beyond its wealth.

A South American colony would thrive,
Prosper and keep Scottish wealth alive,
But the plan soon failed, and Scotland was broke,
So louder voices of reason soon spoke.

By two Acts of Union, both parliaments agreed,
That union as one could only lead,
To greater strength and prosperity,
Paving the way for posterity.

By seventeen 0-seven, both nations had signed,
The Acts which would join and bind,
England and Scotland as one great state,
Together as one to share the same fate.

During all this, Anne had known,
How important it was and had shown,
An interest in how affairs were pursued,
Showing an intellect that was shrewd.

Yet she also had time to spare for art,
A patron to many from her reign's start,
With poetry, theatre and music as well,
Supported that their fame might swell.

Newton was knighted and Handel was granted,
Money that seeds of culture be planted,
As Anne acknowledged art's unique role,
Of describing the world and warming the soul.

But the death of Anne's husband in seventeen 0-8,
Along with age and putting on weight,
Finally led to her being unable,
To even walk without looking unstable.

For several more years, Anne's health decreased,
Whilst the worries of those around did not cease.
In seventeen fourteen, she had the death blow,
When a fatal stroke laid her low.

Many believed that death was her release,
From the pressure and tragedy that didn't cease,
From a life of losing and missing each child,
Of the grief that Anne had not reconciled.

The House of Hanover

Interesting Fact:

The house was formed when the Duchy of Brunswick-Luneburg was divided due to inheritance, and George, the sixth son of the Duke of Brunswick-Luneburg, inherited the Principality of Calenberg and moved his residence to Hanover.

George I
(1714-1727)

Interesting Fact:

When he was crowned king, over twenty towns across the country rioted, such was the disapproval of many people to him being chosen as the monarch.

As the second cousin of Queen Anne,
With the act of settlement placing a ban,
On a Catholic being allowed to succeed,
The choice of George was agreed.

The act of settlement had stipulated,
That Catholic claims must be frustrated,
When someone thought they could inherit,
The throne regardless of any merit.

George was protestant and the only one,
Entitled to follow by schemes which were spun,
By Parliament fearing Catholic rule,
Afraid such a king would be Rome's tool.

George was a German, but qualified,
For England's crown and wasn't denied,
The title of King though some resented,
The protestant front this presented.

Some in England and Scotland tried,
To rebel and for another cried,
A Catholic and Queen Anne's half-brother,
With the prospect of factions fighting each other.

But the rebel plans were slow and bad,
So, they lost any chance they ever had,
Failing to move or decide fast enough,
Defeat came soon, though they weren't treated rough.

But George also had German estates,
Which caused so many lively debates,
As many said that they were concerned,
That George more for Germany yearned.

His rule in Hanover was absolute,
With nobody there who would dispute,
His right to make each big decision,
Allowing him to rule with precision.

As King of England, George was aware,
That power and rule he'd have to share,
With a parliament who embraced,
Government which in freedom was based.

It was under George that Britain first saw,
A better position which would draw,
Upon MP's who were elected,
For skills and ability then selected.

In seventeen twenty-one, to guide MP's,
These men who were the nation's trustees,
The role of Prime Minister was introduced,
With greater efficiency being produced.

Robert Walpole was initiated,
As the one whose power was concentrated,
To help reduce those powers so abused,
Though the title Prime Minister wasn't used.

This all came about due to chaos caused,

By people investing sums without pause,

Into the South Sea Company deal,

Which some thought so good, and some thought unreal.

The price of shares quickly rose,

As cash was invested so others chose,

To float bogus companies to defraud,

Though soon people saw the scheme was flawed.

The Bubble Act had to be passed,

Share prices halted, so people sold fast,

So those who'd bought whilst shares were high,

Could only grieve as plans went awry.

Though George's private life wasn't charmed,

As relations with his son were harmed,

Because George, his son, was liked far more,

Than the King who many thought a bore.

The Prince of Wales sought to gain,
People's praise whilst his father seemed plain,
And even the birth of a son would convince,
Still more to support the popular Prince.

For the King chose a duke which the prince hated,
As baptismal sponsor with tensions created,
Until the Prince insulted the duke,
Which the King only saw as the son's rebuke.

Tension between the King and son soared,
Their cold relations never thawed,
The prince seen by some as the best proposition,
For the King's increasing opposition.

As the years passed by, the King's reputation,
Seemed to suffer continued deflation,
With his German roots and mistresses too,
A storm of criticism blew.

But many thought that George ruled well,
Whose enlightened ways would always tell,
And George was even willing to dare,
To give refuge to the exiled Voltaire.

But the pressure of ruling left its mark,
Left George hurt by critique and remark,
When in seventeen twenty-seven came death,
After a stroke claimed his last breath.

George II (1727-1760)

Interesting Fact:

When his father died, George decided not to go to the funeral in Germany, which proved very popular with his English subjects as they believed it proved he preferred England to Germany. George also overturned his father's will as it threatened to harm the succession to the throne.

Like his father before, he was born,
In Hanover but then was torn,
Away to England when his father became,
King of England to great acclaim.

Then the son stepped up to take,
England's crown for his dynasty's sake,
Though George the Second was a different man,
As more love for England through him ran.

The role of King was different by far,
As Parliament was now allowed to bar,
Things which a monarch might want to do,
A concept the Hanovers thought very new.

For in Hanover George could reign supreme,
Even if his ideas were extreme,
But in England the Houses of Parliament would,
Challenge their King if they felt they should.

So, George left domestic policy to,
MP's whose control over England grew,
But he could return to Germany, where,
His absolute rule found expression there.

Though George was not a King to sit by,
When England raised the battle cry,
Leading his army to fight a war,
That shook parts of Europe to the core.

The War of the Austrian Succession started,
When a Habsburg emperor from life departed,
With Maria Theresa, his daughter, stating,
She was the rightful heir in waiting.

Maria Theresa had the backing,
Of Britain and others who were not lacking,
In giving this Austrian princess assistance,
Though France would offer her resistance.

For eight long years, nations were plunged,
Into campaigns where armies lunged,
Each determined to win and to prove,
The truth of their cause and doubt to remove.

During this war George clearly showed,
How courage through his body flowed,
When, at Dettingen, the foe was faced,
The last English king in battle placed.

In seventeen forty-five there came,
News that rebels had lit the flame,
In Scotland for The Old Pretender,
Raising the rebels to be George's contender.

Another attempt by the Stuarts to break,
Their time in exile and thereby retake,
The crown which James the Second had lost,
Which the Jacobites wanted at any cost.

With so many English troops away,
Fighting in the European fray,
The Jacobite forces fought and won,
Keys battles and made their enemies run.

With many Scottish clans by his side,
It seemed Charles Stuart had turned the tide,
With word being spread they'd get French support,
For all the battles further south they fought.

When they reached Derby, panic spread,
Filling the southern counties with dread,
As it looked as if the Stuarts just might,
Prove by their victory that they were right.

In London, authorities did their best,
To calm the people during this test,
Whilst some loyal subjects penned a song,
'God Save the King' to keep morale strong.

But the Jacobite leadership was divided,
Not enough purpose was provided,
With some not sure where they should be led,
So, they decided to retreat instead.

This retreat north only served to give,
The rule of George its chance to live,
And in April of seventeen forty-six,
The Jacobite leaders ran out of tricks.

For England's army, though weakened and straining,
Received more men and better training,
Chasing the rebels who in time were found,
At Culloden and there beat into the ground.

Once this rebellion had been crushed,
English forces quickly rushed,
To the Scottish Highlands there to pursue,
Persecution of rebels and whoever they knew.

All the while, George had to deal,
With family problems that made him feel,
His son, Frederick, was beginning to be,
Not the kind of person he wanted to see.

His son was the centre for those who desired,
Improvement and change and never tired,
In opposing the King and those he supported,
Doing their best to see George's plans thwarted.

But in seventeen fifty-one fate struck,
The plans for succession came unstuck,
When Frederick died and would leave,
His son and all the nation to grieve.

When George was crowned, Frederick remained,
In Hanover for years with little explained,
So, when the prince was suddenly lost,
The father was left to count the cost.

Though George, when prince, was a popular man,
As the tide of dislike for his father ran,
But once he was King, the unpopular tide,
Was something from which he just couldn't hide.

His frequent trips back to Hanover had,
Caused feelings to him which were often bad,
With rumours spread by his son he was dying,
So, George had to prove his son was lying.

It was also known that George had affairs,
Though Caroline, his wife, wasn't caught unawares,
As George kept his wife well informed,
Of all the liaisons which were performed.

When Caroline died, to George she said,
He must take another wife to his bed,
Yet George heard her words, but never remarried,
With no new wife over threshold carried.

With wife and son both in the grave,
George did all he could to save,
The succession and his dynasty too,
For without a plan plots might accrue.

Prince Frederick had a son of his own,
Born in England, raised and grown,
As an English prince and though still young,
The mantle of Prince of Wales was hung.

When Frederick died, his grandfather wept,
Showing love that was there but only slept,
But now the grandson would be endowed,
With all the trappings his role allowed.

Then in seventeen fifty-six there came,
War with France who many would blame,
For her aggression and her greed,
Who seemed to like watching Europe bleed.

With the island of Minorca invaded,
The people of Britain were soon persuaded,
This act of war by France must be met,
Or else watch her power grow with regret.

For seven long years the war would wage,
With American colonies also the stage,
Of battles to see who'd gain it all,
Of who'd get to see the other one fall.

Early defeats on land and at sea,
Would make the English crave victory,
And a greater effort to win would lead,
The armies and navies of George to succeed.

Even India was not left alone,
With ships of war to her shores blown,
Where, at Arcot and Plassey, Robert Clive,
Won and kept England's interests alive.

A miracle year was in fifty-nine,

With French defeats showing the sign,

Of how the war was going to go,

Each dent to French pride meant England's would grow.

Yet George was already sick and ailing,

Almost deaf and his eyesight failing,

And in seventeen-sixty, his life expired,

After he, to the toilet, had retired.

George III
(1760-1820)

Interesting Fact:

Contrary to accepted thoughts of the time of what a proper gentleman should be and do, George never took a mistress in all the long years of his marriage, and, together with his wife Charlotte, had fifteen children.

Unlike those two Georges before him,
Whose knowledge of English was so slim,
This time the King had been born and raised,
In England and so his birthright was praised.

English, from birth, was then taught,
As more integration had been sought,
With hope that his rule would contain,
Affection and love from the people attain.

Though his father was German, he never went,
To Hanover to rule, but others were sent,
Being content to stay near to home,
Seldom choosing to tour or to roam.

He did his best to hide his roots,
Hiding those German attributes,
To focus on being a true English man,
To show how English blood through him ran.

His mother had taught him to be strict,
So, a virtuous, moral life was picked,
With George always frowning on those who strayed,
When a decadent life by some was displayed.

In the autumn of seventeen sixty-one,
Plans came about which had begun,
To have Charlotte of Mecklenburg-Strelitz arrive,
To marry so that the line might thrive.

They were wed and crowned together,
Neither questioning nor asking whether,
This was a match they'd come to regret,
But together, for decades, their love was set.

A sign of their love and their affection,
That theirs was a deep and strong connection,
Were the fifteen children which they had,
Which, to their bond, would only add.

At first, the King was welcomed by most,
As he was a King who was proud to boast,
That he'd never once set foot abroad,
An English king to support and applaud.

At the start of his reign George knew too well,
The crown estates strain would eventually tell,
So, he sold the lands to the government, who,
Paid an annuity as the civil list grew.

Charities too would receive their share,
Of support from a King who knew how to care,
With lots of annual income donated,
As and when the need dictated.

The Royal Academy of Arts would receive,
Support from George so they could achieve,
Greater status and to reach new heights,
As George was a man who enjoyed those sights.

George was a King who enjoyed to learn,
In an age when gentlemen would daily yearn,
For what new discovery had been found,
To listen to theories that some would expound.

His love of science was known to all,
And often people would shout and call,
'Farmer George' out of respect and praise,
For a King whose life would please and amaze.

It was apt that in his reign began,
An industrial revolution that ran,
Throughout the nation bringing much change,
New ideas which many thought strange.

Where once the products were made by hand,
And most of the labour was tied to the land,
The speed with which things were now produced,
Meant change and uncertainty were introduced.

But his love of science would be a distraction,
The joy of discovery a great attraction,
Allowing George to think and ponder,
About the world and each great wonder.

When a comet was seen in the night sky,
Which, over centuries, often passed by,
George would wonder of future generations,
Of how different the people and their expectations.

He created a library where scholars could sit,
Like minded men of intelligence, wit,
Who wanted to learn and expand their minds,
To study, explore and to share their finds.

During his reign, government was more,
Constitutional than anyone ever saw,
With the Houses of Parliament being more brisk,
In making decisions but accepting the risk.

But the Seven Years War was waging still,
With most of the people having had its fill,
Of war and tax and the effects on trade,
Wishing that plans for peace were made.

In Paris in seventeen sixty-three,
A treaty of peace would let people see,
That trade, at last, could be resumed,
The country's wealth not further consumed.

By this peace, Britain had acquired,
North American lands to which she aspired.
George then decreed what he thought was best,
Banning the colonists from expanding west.

He believed the tribes needed his protection,
With trade in furs needing better direction,
So, he declared what he thought was just,
With the rights of tribes not turning to dust.

For most of his life, George resided,
In southern England, though sometimes decided,
To take the waters in a seaside town,
In Weymouth in Dorset when he was down.

Yet, trouble across the sea would arise,
Which, to some, came as no surprise,
When the American colonies objected,
To paying a tax which Parliament selected.

Ministers in London held the view,
That as colonies prospered and they grew,
Those living there should have to pay,
When protecting armies were sent their way.

Those in the colonies then declared,
That decisions on taxes should be shared,
But no one was there who could represent,
The colonial thoughts or fury vent.

Without representation, the colonies felt,
Their voices weren't heard, and they'd been dealt,
A terrible set back until parliament approved,
That all tax, bar for tea, should be removed.

Then in Boston in seventeen seventy-three,
Ships which were there carrying tea,
Were entered and chests were dumped overboard,
In an act of defiance to strike a chord.

In no time at all, things escalate,
With colonies and Britain entering a state,
Of outright war against one another,
Enemies where once they were friends and brother.

The rebels fought for what they believed,
Were rights infringed and must be retrieved,
Seeing themselves as English men still,
Fighting oppression and preparing to kill.

At this time, George gave his backing,
To his leaders in England who were attacking,
The rebels who were seen as betraying,
Law and order by what they were saying.

A petition to George was quickly rejected,
His position against the rebels selected,
And soon the bloody course would be set,
When troops at Lexington and Concord were met.

At Bunker Hill the shots were fired,
By which both sides were quickly mired.
The redcoats stormed the rebels hill,
And forced to swallow a bitter pill.

Rebellion had but little hope,
With English might and wealth to cope.
The rebel troops were not out paced,
But, often from the contest chased.

In the trees, or course of the river,
Young volunteers would crouch and shiver.
Irregular troops would try their hand,
At making their fight fierce and grand.

The redcoats often had they prey,
Where one more push might victory sway.
Colonials had rebellion dared,
Yet, every time so badly fared.

Redcoat skill at arms had told,
But rebel moves were rash and bold.
Washington's troops from success were banned,
As his ragged regiments were thinly manned.

Colonials faced constant disaster,
And defeat crept up ever faster.
The darkest days were filled with gloom,
As each foresaw impending doom.

When all seemed done, and all hard pressed,
When all, for home, were sad and obsessed,
The French were drawn to speak and prance,
Aware of England's circumstance.

In time, the lessons of war were applied,
When rebels fought well, learnt not to hide.
Now redcoats faced a foe so strange,
Whose skill took on a broader range.

What most had thought would end with ease,
Had thought the end their king would please,
Soon showed the plan now had a flaw,
Would shake old England to the core.

Beset with foes now all around,
Intent on forcing English ground,
England's power had been abused,
As all her chances had been used.

Once Yorktown and its army quit,
A mortal blow had now been hit,
To keeping the thirteen colonies,
Or keeping imperial sympathies.

In time, the King would learn to accept,
The loss of the colonies for which he wept,
Meeting John Adams of the United States,
To acknowledge he'd now accepted their fates.

Thousands of slaves on farm and plantation,
Escaped the suffering and privation,
To fight former masters and to serve,
For freedom to show they had the nerve.

For a long time, George had seen and known,
How the trade in slaves had prospered and grown,
To become a business towards which,
Many had turned to become very rich.

Like any man who felt enlightened,
He saw how this evil trade had tightened,
Like a noose around society's neck,
Which would be the end if without check.

There were those who already said,
That a more humane path must be led,
To put an end to the exploitation,
Of those who were also God's creation.

In eighteen 0-seven, George would sign,
The legal document that would consign,
The transatlantic trade of each slave,
To banishment and its eventual grave.

Yet, despite all the setbacks and the threats,
Most of the people had few regrets,
About their King, who they so admired,
For devotion to marriage which never tired.

In an age when husbands were expected to stray,
George chose devotion which he chose to display,
But this wouldn't save him for what was to follow,
An illness which left a whole man hollow.

Others had noticed that something was there,
Mild at first, not enough to scare,
Though later in life, it would manifest,
Into something that would all Britain test.

Eccentric behaviour which would fill,
Daily routines and eventually spill,
Into the court and government too,
Then it passed and things were like new.

Yet then came a crisis to focus each mind,
A threat to all of a different kind,
When people in France had had enough,
After years of being treated so rough.

Protests soon became revolution,
With fanatics set on one resolution,
That of clear and fundamental change,
The ways of the past to rearrange.

In time, the king of France was beheaded,
Which every monarch in Europe dreaded,
So then more war with France begins,
But rebel zeal gave them early wins.

By going to war, they made a distraction,
Which helped shore up their radical faction.
Britain's navy was more than a match,
For any old sail, her skippers might catch.

Her maritime trade was the nation's lifeline,
Allowing her people to trade and dine.
From British trade, an empire was wrought,
Where status and power might yet be bought.

Yet, the war with France had gone against them,
Though, Britain was known for her pluck and phlegm.
Napoleon's troops fought like men in a trance,
Led him to Victory's glorious dance.

Britain sent armies to deliver a blow.
While generals would dance, toast and crow.
Together, they'd make the enemy bleat,
But lost the day, and withdrawal was discreet.

To turn this war, great plans were seeded,
As victories at sea, and on land were needed.
Nelson and Wellesley would not fail,
French opposition and might to scale.

Both would choose their special site,
To put an end to Europe's plight.
They, in turn, would heal those sores,
Win posterity's loud applause.

Nelson was the first to act,

Had never skill and daring lacked.

He longed to feel the battle's heat,

And the French in mortal combat meet.

Trafalgar was a scene so tragic,

Where Nelson's tars performed such magic.

Caught the enemy in deep water,

Then gave the word to give them slaughter.

Even as the ships were locked,

Nelson all the danger mocked.

He strode the deck as if walking his hall,

Until a sniper planted his ball.

A Sniper's shot struck him fast.

Death from atop the rigging was cast.

Nelson stood through shot and shell,

And on his deck, he mortally fell.

Alive but wounded, he was carried below,
Afraid his wound might cause them woe.
He fought the pain 'til near expended,
'Til Britain's freedom had been defended.

Britain's navy ruled the wave.
Her wooden ships would liberty save.
Her foe's defeat was cruelly felt,
As the cannon's smoke by all was smelt.

But, fledgling America, with diplomacy's grin,
Wanted the Empire's reason to win.
America spoke and plainly insisted,
That attacks on her trade be duly resisted.

For Britain's ships attacked with impunity,
All foreign ships without any scrutiny.
Britain hoped her power to enhance,
Without a care or second glance.

America threatened with all her tact,
If Britain didn't face the fact,
That America needed her foreign dues,
And British aggression would light the war's fuse.

But Britain could not yet allow,
Foreign trade in French seas to plough.
So, war with America soon was started,
As diplomatic ways departed.

Frigates engaged, and signals flashed,
As waves 'gainst hulls battered and splashed.
Americans gazed with a worried frown,
While the redcoats, at last, burnt Washington town.

However, Napoleon wasn't yet quite through,
And allied hopes for winning undue.
He still posed a threat to all humanity,
Still tainted the world with his profanity.

Napoleon, to France, wasn't everything,
Yet, to liberty, equality they'd gladly cling.
A threat to establishment was still clearly posed,
Awakening all the powers that dozed.

On land, his genius wasn't beat.
Excelling in the military feat.
But his power by Russian snow was cropped,
For a while, the threat to Europe was stopped.

To restore France's power, an army was massed,
Napoleon, once more, a monster was classed.
So, a man with great skill was sought to lead,
A coalition force to make France bleed.

Wellesley had fought the French across Spain,
Had fought across mountain, through heat and rain.
He was given control and given freehand,
And to crush the French was their one demand.

Napoleon hadn't lost the spell,
Of making nations together gel.
They knew this was his last 'hurrah',
But he caught them cold at Quatre Bras.

Allied plans were forced to alter,
As Napoleon hoped their resolve would falter.
The allies wondered what to do,
As their forces closed at Waterloo.

In Belgium, the allied plans resigned,
Here their regiments would be lined.
Their coalition force would wait,
For the French to come and take the bait.

Europe had known a war so bloody.
Clouds of war had lingered so ruddy.
The war had shown that they had the will,
To endure the war and pay the bill.

But by eighteen ten, George was ailing,
Had rheumatic pain with eyesight failing,
Then his mental illness became severe,
Which left the role of King unclear.

So, in eighteen eleven, it was agreed,
That a Regency government should be decreed,
By which his son, George, would take,
The role of King and decisions make.

For the rest of his life, the King would remain,
At Windsor Castle, either ill or insane,
Then in eighteen twenty, death descended,
His torment and pain finally ended.

George IV (1820-1830)

Interesting Fact:

Whilst a great supporter of the arts, the latest styles and manners, George gained a bad reputation with the people for his extravagance and the way he treated his wife. When he died, The Times wrote: 'there never was an individual less regretted by his fellow creatures than this deceased king.'

The first gentleman of England had,
Thought of his father as old and mad,
So, when the Regency Act was announced,
He, and his people, were quick to pounce.

Before he was crowned, the Regent displayed,
A love of pleasure and was often arrayed,
In extravagant clothes to show his passion,
For the beauty of the latest fashion.

His circle of friends were those he trusted,
To follow his path and to whims adjusted,
Depending on how they caught his mood,
Which left others thinking he was quite lewd.

The regency era was full of fun,
For a prince that was able to easily shun,
The advice of those who could see ahead,
To a time when the King was finally dead.

Yet his love of life and culture made,
A contribution that wouldn't fade,
With the Royal Pavilion in Brighton designed,
Windsor Castle and Buckingham Palace refined.

Caroline of Brunswick, his German wife,
Led a sad and unfortunate life,
Neglected by George who didn't hide,
He had no love for his foreign bride.

For George had been married years ago,
To Maria Fitzherbert, but couldn't show,
As the marriage, by law, was seen as illegal,
So was kept very quiet and not very regal.

Caroline and George had an only child,
But duty done, now free to run wild,
George could return to what he loved best,
Women, wine and a flash suit and vest.

The people loved Caroline more than him,
So, attempts to divorce at a whim,
Were dropped as the people were outraged,
That such an attempt on her would be staged.

The people didn't want to have this rake,
As king for fears that he would take,
More liberties with his newfound riches,
Wasting it all on wine and britches.

Scandal had followed George all his days,
With little sign he'd mend his ways,
And not even when the crown was gained,
Were appetites lost or simply restrained.

He seemed to be ruled by favourites, who,
We free to speak and say as they do,
Leading George this way or that,
Depending on where their interests sat.

The government saw him as selfish, unreliable,
His irresponsibility undeniable,
So, getting the work of governing done,
Was a task and always enjoyed by none.

A staunch anti-Catholic, he hadn't approved,
When more restrictions had been removed,
To give Catholics more emancipation,
Believing the religion an abomination.

Then something happened to raise a cheer,
When war with France, which cost them dear,
Finally ended with Napoleon's defeat,
At Waterloo, with victory complete.

But a life of excess was catching up,
Of drinking too much from that privileged cup,
So, as he got older, diseases set in,
Which many put down to a life full of sin.

Blindness and gout, his doctors said,
Were painful enough to keep him in bed,
With laudanum taken to ease the pain,
That he could indulge to excess yet again.

This gentleman dandy put on more weight,
A slave to his passions and so to fate,
For a life of indulgence was bound to tell,
As courtiers watched his body swell.

By June eighteen thirty, the end was in sight,
His body large and a painful sight,
And it wasn't long before it refused,
To keep him alive after being abused.

His only child, Charlotte, hadn't survived,
So direct succession from George was deprived,
With a younger brother also departed,
Another brother's line was started.

William IV
(1830-1837)

Interesting Fact:

Marrying late in life, William had no surviving legitimate children, but did have ten children with his mistress the actress Dorothea Jordan, with whom he lived for twenty years.

Here was a prince who never supposed,
He'd be a king when the thought was proposed,
But due to the hand of fickle fate,
He'd got the crown, though somewhat late.

Already in his sixties when,
By proclamation and sweep of the pen,
William took his brother's throne,
Though youthful vigour had already flown.

As a young man he'd gladly served,
In the Royal Navy and well deserved,
The praise of officers and men alike,
As one who was keen to engage and strike.

He rose to command his very own ship,
A fast little frigate that would slip,
From port to port with a prince as its master,
A competent skipper who avoided disaster.

Nelson himself was once in command,
Of a ship where he took the prince in hand,
Becoming friends once their paths had crossed,
So, William mourned when Nelson was lost.

But that was all many years in the past,
When his days were full of sail and mast,
Yet here he was for all to behold,
The once youthful sailor turned King, but old.

His reign would be short, but would see,
The Act of eighteen thirty-three,
Where slavery in the empire would end,
As it was something not to defend.

The British empire was free to expand,
And business quickly placed its brand.
Its dreams of wealth, it would safely nest,
As world domination was covertly dressed.

The demand for goods soon gathered pace,
And convenience soon was commonplace.
Mass production from industrial revolution,
Created a global institution.

The poor laws too were taken in hand,
The existing system not able to stand,
Until the law changed the administration,
To ways that became an abomination.

For the rest of the century, and into the next,
The poor were exposed to workhouse affects,
Treated as if they alone were the cause,
Of all the suffering without pause.

Though in politics, William always tried,
To take the scheming in his stride,
Unlike his father or brother who showed,
They ruled as King by a different code.

It was late in life when William thought,
A suitable wife should be sought,
With Adelaide of Saxe-Meiningen picked,
To whom his fidelity was always strict.

But William had not missed the chance,
Of finding someone to experience romance,
Loving Dorothea, an actress who cared,
Not married but living a love they shared.

Over the years, ten children were born,
But two, by death, were from them torn,
Leaving the eight which laws didn't permit,
To rule as they were illegitimate.

In eighteen thirty-seven, the issue arose,
Of who'd succeed and the problems they'd pose,
As the fear was that on the King's decease,
All that was left was a very young niece.

Victoria (1837-1901)

Interesting Fact:

Victoria reigned longer than any other monarch before her. What's more, she was the first British monarch to ever be photographed, giving us a true image of what she looked like. She was also the first monarch to take up residence at Buckingham Palace.

At just eighteen when she achieved,

The crown of England and received,

Title of Queen which some had not,

Thought would happen or be her lot.

Many believed she was too obscure,

Though now her claim was seen as pure,

Being the former King's next of kin,

His niece whose claims were not too thin.

Alexandrina Victoria was her name,

Though she would gain better fame,

When her name Alexandrina was dropped,

When she chose just the first to adopt.

As Queen Victoria, she tried to rule,

Trying not to be anyone's fool,

But the intrigues of court soon arose,

With courtiers and ministers treading on toes.

When the mother of one of her ladies in waiting,
Fell pregnant, or so some others were stating,
The Queen fell foul for the way she treated,
The falsely accused with talk being heated.

The lady was thought to be pregnant but,
The diagnosis was not clean cut,
For upon inspection, a tumour was found,
And Victoria's words by the mob were drowned.

Victoria did try to help and shape,
The court proceedings and the red tape,
Which stated the government were allowed,
To pick ladies in waiting who to them were avowed.

But Victoria stated she'd choose her own,
Whose loyalty only to her were known,
Not wanting to give the government spies,
Not wanting those ladies with government ties.

Just three years into her reign she fell,
Under her first cousin's loving spell,
Prince Albert who she chose to wed,
All fear and apprehension fled.

Albert would be the love of her life,
She would be his loving wife,
Together as one and the nation smiled,
Each time the Queen gave birth to a child.

Confidant, lover and best friend,
Together they were a perfect blend,
Of friendship, passion and a deep love,
To which they gave thanks to God above.

But not long after, a plan was laid,
To kill the Queen and the attempt was made,
Whilst she and Albert were in a carriage,
Just months into their loving marriage.

The man who tried the assassination,
Sought the couple's annihilation,
Failed to kill them, and the nation gasped,
With a new love for Victoria grasped.

Though Albert wasn't crowned or permitted,
To rule as a king he was still committed,
To showing the nation that he cared,
His zeal and his energy not being spared.

He was instrumental in the creation,
Of the Great Exhibition, where each nation,
Could come and show what they had to offer,
What the great minds of the age could proffer.

All the nations of world civilisation,
Flocked to see the latest sensation.
The world would show its latest wares,
To great applause and wondrous stares.

The future of man was now on display,
Where nations showed how invention could pay.
They saw inventions of the highest grade,
From mechanical feats to the finest braid.

Capitalism seemed like a glorious saint,
Whose wealth and ambition couldn't possibly taint.
But the poor lived in cities where disease often dwelt,
Where death, beside them, in prayer always knelt.

The gap between the classes was wide.
The poor would have their time to bide.
Knowing one's station was the order of things,
So, they ignored the evils that poverty brings.

Some saw this squalor with their very own eyes,
Saw all the slums and heard the loud sighs,
Of mothers with children crying for bread,
Who lived each day by the thinnest of thread.

Charles Dickens was one who'd written a book,
That exposed the evils of squalor and nook.
It helped people see that they couldn't ignore,
The terrible veil that poverty wore.

British wealth and the upper classes,
Were built upon the lowly masses.
People wanted the system reformed,
Saw society as unjust, and deformed.

Industrial barons tried to quell,
The hope that unions tried to sell.
The barons focused on increasing their net,
Worried that quotas wouldn't be met.

Many were hopeful and keen to show,
That this evil they knew as the status quo,
Was relentless and always was unceasing,
That faith in society was forever decreasing.

Then Reason spoke with a voice indignant,
To challenge the system that thrived malignant.
Reform, slowly, came out in front,
And it, to Reason, could merely grunt.

Many believed it was a great waste,
Of money and time spent in haste,
With Ireland still suffering from a great starvation,
The Potato Famine with all its privation.

But the Queen had already given much aid,
To Ireland's poor who had clearly paid,
The price for those who owned the land,
Bad landlords who for profit planned.

She was also keen to improve relations,
Between those former warring nations,
Britain and France and so she went,
To France with hope and good intent.

In eighteen fifty-three, war in Crimea,
Would foster this entente idea,
As Britain and France went to war as allies,
Against Russia and so confirmed those ties.

But the war would highlight just how unprepared,
Britain's forces were once war was declared,
With the battles proving bloody and hard,
With little shown for the soldier's regard.

Many would suffer before there was change,
Before tactics and attitudes would rearrange,
Until women like Florence Nightingale said,
She'd go to the aid of all those who bled.

With improvement in hospitals and in the field,
The Russian foe would slowly yield,
With France and Britain both pushing on,
In a closer and more open liaison.

Yet, despite all the trappings of holding court,
Peace by Victoria and Albert were sought,
At the house they bought on the Isle of Wight,
At Osborne where they could stay out of sight.

The loving couple would share much time,
At Osborne away from London's grime,
At a place for a family which was fine,
A family whose children numbered nine.

Then came disaster for the family and nation,
Which left the Queen in desperation,
When Albert died of typhoid fever,
Not thinking her husband would ever leave her.

Devastated by this terrible loss,
Over which no words of comfort could gloss,
Victoria began to wear nothing but black,
Lost in mourning and would never come back.

For the rest of her life, she would miss,
Her partner, soul mate, and his sweet kiss,
Putting all other cares aside,
No longer with him but death's dark bride.

She tried to keep herself far away,
From people and would only stay,
In her favourite places to avoid the gaze,
Of a nation that lost its royal praise.

She began to rely more and more,
On those close around to help her restore,
Some sort of sanity and peace of mind,
With one in particular appearing too kind.

John Brown was a servant who, some implied,
Had married the Queen in secret, or tried,
To become much more above his station,
Which she accepted without hesitation.

Victoria had always liked to record,
Events in her life which were stored,
In diaries which would often show,
How her mind and feelings would flow.

Later, the Queen would publish a book,
Which then allowed the reader to look,
Into her mind and where, quite unshyly,
She speaks of John Brown so very highly.

Later in life, she'd find this again,
From a servant who helped ease her pain,
Of feeling alone and still living in grief,
Getting comfort and help from the servant's belief.

Abdul Karim was an Indian who,
Held his Muslim beliefs to be true,
And Victoria held this man to be dear,
Always wanting her 'Munshi' to be near.

But she knew the running of Britain would need,
Her input if government were to succeed,
With a long list of ministers having to deal,
With the Queen and all her ways so surreal.

Over the years, and despite her grief,
She'd meet prime ministers who felt relief,
Once they had escaped from her gloom,
No longer having to share the same room.

Victoria would see a rapid change,
To social laws which would rearrange,
How society treated the many poor,
Saw the improvement in social law.

Much of what changed left many unnerved,
Fearing the system which they had served,
Afraid that the common man would acquire,
More wealth and say as hopes rose higher.

Yet she also saw the empire's increase,
With the nation, it seemed, hardly ever at peace,
As factions in government sought to expand
On opportunities that were at hand.

India, Africa and Asia as well,
Would see the redcoats or the ship's swell,
As imperial forces in London agreed,
Some part of the world had Britain's need.

In Victoria's reign, the empire ruled,
So much of the globe that children were schooled,
In believing that Britain's rule was best,
That all subject peoples should feel blessed.

Britain looked strong, both home and abroad,
Of enlarging the empire, she never got bored.
A navy was built to race under sail,
To serve the empire through calm and through gale.

At home, there was progress in reason and learning,
Gone were all plots and rebellious yearning.
Knowledge and trade were fashionable then,
Where gentlemen used not the sword but the pen.

A time when technology was sought to progress,
The advancement of man from all ignorant mess.
To enlighten the world by the strength of knowledge,
A place where the rich were enlightened in college.

With money and wisdom England would change,
To stately homes with their gardens and grange.
A land that was seeking on itself to improve,
In industry, learning, and chaos to remove.

Britain wanted a status to gain,
To build the magnificent, ignorance to drain.
On the edge of a world, new and exciting,
The British were confident, ambitious, inviting.

With the passion for knowledge set in their mind,
The British, for novelty, longed for and pined.
Everyday life was changed by invention,
While the poor suffered still by the good intention.

The fires of industry were fiercely coaxed,
As cities grew and were quickly choked.
People to the cities flocked,
And air and rivers were quickly blocked.

British goods had a quality achieved,
Were well made and gladly received.
Her reputation soared to the sky,
As demand outstripped all supply.

All this power came from the workers,
But the tired poor were seen as shirkers.
Industrialists grew rich and fat,
Whilst people, in their squalor, sat.

There grew a gap between rich and poor,
That ate the mass like some cancerous maw.
Some would try this wound to tend,
The ways of society would have to mend.

But social reform would fuel a thought,
Which left imperialism very distraught,
As republican sentiments began to stir,
As the lines of oppression began to blur.

Both home and abroad, people were thinking,
The line of morality was quickly shrinking,
With many poor people no more than slaves,
Whilst British ships still ruled the waves.

London itself had seen a rise,
In the number of people and its size,
As industry grew and wealth was sort,
In the great metropolis and its port.

The same had happened in other places,
Cities in Britain filled with the faces,
Of hopeful people with families in tow,
Working in squalor and watching slums grow.

Wages were low and hours were long,
Yet the factory owners didn't see any wrong,
In letting the children work for a pittance,
Keen to exploit and allow their admittance.

And not far from home, some nations believed,
A direct challenge should be conceived,
As France and Germany both contested,
More wealth in them should be invested.

The mood of nations was always shifting,
Loyalties to their allies drifting,
With a German economy getting strong,
United and by its dreams borne along.

Tension with France and Germany grew,
With the belief which most people knew,
That war would come, but when and where,
Nobody knew or how they would fare.

For some of the children Victoria had,
Were married to families so they could add,
More ties to Britain to help sustain,
Closer relations in each domain.

Her and Albert's nine children produced,
Forty-two grandchildren with some introduced,
As brides for princes as they were worth,
As much for their parentage as giving birth.

From these marriages, both near and far,
Would come a Kaiser and a Tsar,
Both linked to Britain by their mothers,
Related and looking like they were brothers.

At the heart of it all sat the great Queen,
Controlling, elegant with a strict routine,
Which her children and offspring felt oppressive,
Still dark and mourning and very depressive.

When the grandchildren in time became,
Kings of their nations it was still the same,
With their grandmother still at the heart,
Of how they would rule and could never depart.

Even when Germany was in competition,
The Kaiser pushed on by his ambition,
He wondered what his grandmother might think,
Her presence keeping the world from the brink.

The Queen, though ageing and putting on weight,
Was loved by those who would celebrate,
The length of her reign through jubilees,
Which, difficult for her, were meant to please.

First Golden and then Diamond too,
Were occasions when the crowds could renew,
Their appreciation and their gratitude,
For pride in empire in which they were imbued.

Across the empire, statues were erected,
Officials in towns were also selected,
To organise parties and give a speech,
The pride of empire to all to preach.

Yet Victoria was as reluctant as ever,
To leave her home for this endeavour,
Though convinced it would be for the best,
The reluctant Queen went through with the test.

But even as the parties were held,
In South Africa farmers were being shelled,
By imperial troops who were trying to beat,
The Boers who refused to acknowledge defeat.

Of their cause, the Boers were convinced,
And in taking their land, the British winced.
The men of the empire were convinced by their peers,
Who said they needed to get volunteers.

Yet, technology played a startling card,
As British hopes were stopped and jarred.
Inventions had their weapons changed,
Left the generals unsure, quite deranged.

The Boers had friends from overseas,
Keen to help, British hopes to tease.
They gave the Boer the means to protect,
Equipped them with rifles without defect.

Defeating the Boers proved a great task,
And the empire lost invincibility's mask.
To learn the truth, came as a shock,
Which made the generals sit and take stock.

Casualties mounted; the outcome looked bleak.
And the empire decided a remedy to seek.
Kitchener soon took ultimate control,
Whose tactics would the empire console.

He knew the Boers would take time to crush,
Knew that his forces had to creep not rush.
So, each family was taken to a large, enclosed camp,
Where conditions were evil, unclean, and damp.

There they would wait whilst the war was carried,
To all the commandos, who were tired and harried.
Thousands of women and children would die,
Whilst the empire ignored their lamentable cry.

Just a short while later, in nineteen 0-one,
Her long and magnificent reign was done,
With the Queen and Empress of India ailing,
Her tired and overweight body failing.

Victoria ruled for near sixty-four years,
For most of that time she'd shed many tears,
For Albert's loss from which she could not,
Recover or from her memory blot.

During her reign, the empire had grown,
But the seeds of war had also been sown,
And with her passing the world would change,
Its character different and somehow strange.

The House of Saxe-Coburg & Gotha

Interesting Fact:

Founded in 1826, it is a branch of the Saxon House of Wettin.

Edward VII (1901-1910)

Interesting Fact:

Renowned as a playboy and as someone who liked to enjoy life to the full, Edward very much enjoyed the company of women, having affairs with at least fifty-five from all walks of life and classes of society.

Victoria and Albert's second child,
Whose early years were free and wild,
Bertie, as he was often called,
Sometimes left his mother appalled.

The first male descendant who could define,
The whole Saxe-Coburg and Gotha line,
His early examples would mainly shock,
The whole of high society rock.

Living a life that he would measure,
By its vices and his pleasure,
With excess being his only guide,
Which he didn't try to hide.

The Queen was held in great respect,
While Bertie showed such great neglect,
For all the values his mother held,
Which, to some, disaster spelled.

Women by him were always pursued,
Because to Bertie they were viewed,
As things of beauty, he had to possess,
As part of his life of privileged excess.

Along with drinking and good cigars,
Parties with friends and music hall stars,
He lived his life until he was gorged,
His reputation duly forged.

His wife, Alexandra of Denmark had,
To hear the stories which were bad,
Sordid liaisons and embarrassing tales,
About the playboy Prince of Wales.

Yet he also found the time to aid,
With public appearances that were made,
To show the people, both home and abroad,
What majesty in the royals was stored.

At public events, standing aloof,
With many people knowing the truth,
Most of the people felt a connection,
For the playboy prince who had their affection.

But Queen Victoria was not amused,
With the way her son had abused,
His royal position just to have fun,
A style of living she hoped he'd shun.

Yet once he was king, he began to act,
Much more responsibly and not distract,
From the image of his royal status,
Showed interest in government apparatus.

After the Second Boer War had ended,
Parliament no longer had pretended,
That Britain's forces were the best,
As the Boers had put them to the test.

King Edward helped to modernise,
The Royal Navy in everyone's eyes,
With the army's structure organised,
To higher standards some devised.

Ceremony too played a big part,
In helping his image from the start,
With great events going some way,
To show off tradition through great display.

Bertie would also his time devote,
To visiting countries to promote,
More understanding and a desire,
For peace for which he'd never tire.

To the people of France, he was known,
As 'Peacemaker' for his friendly tone,
And Bertie did have a special place,
In his heart for France and the Gallic race.

He'd spent much time in Paris, where,
The vice he craved was not so rare,
But, as a King, he went to impart,
Words of peace from the start.

An Entente between two nations defined,
How bright the love of peace then shined,
In a mood of mutual admiration,
With Bertie receiving adulation.

Yet a closer tie with France would mean,
A widening gap with others was seen,
Especially with the Kaiser, who,
From the entente conclusions drew.

Kaiser Wilhelm of Germany stood,
The loser of this new brotherhood,
Which saw France and Britain as new friends,
Each, for the past making amends.

As Bertie's nephew, the Kaiser protested,
That so much effort with France be invested,
When Germany was Britain's old ally,
Suddenly left so high and dry.

But Bertie's choice also coincided,
With what he felt and then decided,
For he didn't like his nephew much,
Thought him a brute with a heavy touch.

The Germans were also seen as a threat,
Competition to trade which must be met,
With a growing navy which one day could,
Be used by the Kaiser if up to no good.

The German economy had quickly grown,
Its quality goods soon were shown,
To a world market which could not resist,
The chance to have what could not be missed.

And while the King worked towards,
Much better relations and its rewards,
All the while there were those men,
From humble lives whose sword was the pen.

Socialist reformers who craved revolution,
To change each level of institution,
Men who were keen activists,
Radical thinkers and socialists.

Through past reform, more people achieved,
More education and so perceived,
How badly the wealth was distributed,
Which was to class attributed.

Many believed that women should vote,
But such was their cry that few took note.
So, they turned their hands to violent actions,
In the hope of convincing the ruling factions.

Instead of the vote, they were sent to gaol,
Yet the movement simply would not pale.
Across the land their cause was ranging,
Aware that society was slowly changing.

Hunger strikes and chained to railings,
The women hoped to show the failings,
Of a system that was harsh, unjust,
A society in tradition trussed.

The waters, still, were dark and muddied,
Many would suffer, be bruised and bloodied,
While men could vote as they said it was earnt,
Denying the right for those who weren't.

The need for change was now laid bare,
As life, to many, was seen as unfair.
The difference in classes made people concerned,
Which, for some, was easily discerned.

In an effort to fight it, the government hid,
Their counter forces, and things which they did.
Attending the meetings, speakers were baited,
And for those who spoke out, prison awaited.

Alongside all this, technology too,
Was changing lives and people's view,
Of how society could be improved,
If the old structures could be removed.

But Bertie would not get to see its crash,
Not see the old world turn to ash,
For in nineteen ten, he breathed his last,
His body failed through abuses so vast.

George V
(1910-1936)

Interesting Fact:

Not excelling intellectually, his father believed that service in the Royal Navy would do him the world of good. So, at the tender age of just twelve, George was packed off to cadet training at Dartmouth in Devon.

The son of Edward, George had acquired,
The crown once Bertie's life expired,
With Albert, his older brother, dead,
George would take the throne instead.

As a young man, George had served,
In the navy and thought he deserved,
A simpler life serving aboard,
Ships of the line which he adored.

Once his brother was dead, he found,
Greater pressure was all around,
As he was going to be next in line,
King by fickle fate's design.

His brother Albert was engaged to marry,
Mary of Teck and together carry,
The royal line even further still,
But gaps were left which George would fill.

George and his father, Bertie, were close,
With Bertie his friend and rarely morose,
For they had never had a cross word,
As the spirit of friendship within them stirred.

Not only would he now inherit,
The crown and have to prove his merit,
But he'd also have to marry the bride,
Which Albert planned to have by his side.

Soon after the wedding, a rumour was spread,
Saying George had already taken to bed,
A wife, but George simply laughed it off,
A stupid joke to make people scoff.

Not long after George became,
King and Emperor, he could claim,
To have overseen a momentous change,
Which would British politics rearrange.

For in nineteen eleven, the Parliament Act,
Would enormous attention attract,
As the House of Commons, which was elected,
Had supremacy over the Lords protected.

George also made his views very clear,
When he sought to have Parliament's ear,
Saying he wouldn't speak or attend,
As anti-Catholic words might offend.

Parliament relented and so agreed,
In the modern world there was a need,
To update the speech the King should make,
Passing an Act for tolerance's sake.

George found himself daily surrounded,
By modern ideas and ways which confounded,
The spirit of the old world which he knew,
Watching as the darker spirits grew.

In mainland Europe, political unrest,
Forced Kings and governments to do their best,
In changing their ways or simply to purge,
All those whose views were on the verge.

No one could have seen or foretold,
The way events would go or unfold.
Alliances held at Future's expense,
And a wonderful summer, fearful and tense.

Many in Britain wanted social reform,
To avoid the brewing social storm,
Which was coming and threatened to break,
Upon them all, and much was at stake.

Close to home, there were those who agreed,
The people of Ireland should be freed,
So, they could rule themselves at last,
But events abroad saw that talks didn't last.

In nineteen fourteen, war was declared,

After a nobleman's life wasn't spared,

By an assassin who stepped out from the crowd,

Shots which over the world sounded loud.

Soon, even Britain had been drawn,

Into the war and a new age's dawn,

As alliances forced all Europe to action,

The people swept up by this novel distraction.

Off to war, the Tommies beamed,

Like a great adventure, or so it seemed.

Extremely well trained, but heavily encumbered,

The poor bloody infantry was heavily outnumbered.

Then Germany changed their plan so trusted,

Their right wing moved and slightly adjusted.

This gave the allies the chance they'd longed for,

Allowed them, at last, to strike the Hun's jaw.

All through the empire, men answered the call,

Lest, on Britain, defeat should befall.

From old soldiers to novice, each donned the kit,

And for England and empire, each did their bit.

Such youth and such talent marched in the sun,

As if on adventure filled with such fun.

They marched to the sound of artillery's boom,

Those fresh-faced boys, not long out the womb.

The songs of the war sent men on their way,

As troops were needed to fight and to slay.

'We don't want to lose you, but we think you ought to go,

For your king and your country, both need you so.'

This wasn't a war like those in the past,

And each was afraid that the thrill wouldn't last.

Yet industrial slaughter soon told the tale,

To add to the nation's sad travail.

The Tommies advanced waist deep in mud,
As the land was churned by shell and flood.
Thousands by their adventure consumed.
Bodies left or by shells exhumed.

Ypres, Somme, Passchendaele, Loos,
Tommies fought through the mud and the ooze.
But the generals kept pushing, never would tire,
Of pitting mere flesh against the enemy's wire.

Millions were killed, wounded or missing,
As the hatred played on, animosity hissing.
The empire spewed out its killing machines,
Gave them to boys who were still in their teens.

Questioning whether their cause was humane,
Some would wonder if the world was sane.
A few hurt souls wrote their verse,
Full of anger, judgement, short and terse.

A generation of men would be scarred,

Once talks of peace were constantly barred.

It was obvious to all who served in the trench,

That the German wire in their blood they'd drench.

The Great War would end at a specified hour,

But the peace for the Germans was bitter and sour.

They'd lost the war amidst pain and sobbing,

Then watched as the victors came rejoicing and robbing.

The House of Windsor

Interesting Fact:

In 1917, anti-German feelings were so high in the nation that the royal family decided it would be best to change their German name to something more British sounding.

At the height of the war, George would change,
Those German names which were strange,
To British people who now regarded,
All German connections must be discarded.

But what to choose was a concern,
Though very soon the empire would learn,
That Windsor was the name preferred,
With patriotic feelings stirred.

Once the war was won or lost,
Once nations saw the final cost,
Some got together to try to ensure,
The paths to such folly would not endure.

A League of Nations was conceived,
By those who in man's reason believed,
To try to prevent such wars again,
That nations might not feel such pain.

Yet there were some who'd only discovered,
A different lesson when peace was recovered,
With those who'd felt such a great loss,
To them different lessons had come across.

During the war, the Russians had proved,
That Tsar and government could be removed,
Replacing the old imperial state,
With a communist one which many would hate.

Some had wanted to rescue the Tsar,
While some thought the plan went too far,
As many worried what people might think,
That support for George might rapidly shrink.

The Tsar and his family would remain,
With Bolshevik forces and be slain,
Shot out of hand because they were royal,
Denied a rescue by those who were loyal.

Several monarchs of Europe fell,

Lost to change from out of war's hell,

Replaced by republics or a socialist state,

The thoughts for their king fueled by hate.

George could only try to ride,

The wave of nationalist fervour and pride,

That swept through Europe and the world,

With flags of national parties unfurled.

The question of Ireland rose once more,

As, yet again, many people saw,

It was time for Ireland to be given,

Freedom, for which so many were driven.

In nineteen twenty-two, with London's permission,

Ireland took steps towards her partition,

With the Irish Free State being shaped,

At last, from London's grip escaped.

After the war, a great depression,
Had followed war and the aggression,
Leaving many people almost destitute,
With governments in such disrepute.

Countries like Germany were badly hit,
Its economy after the war barely fit,
To deal with the world's financial mess,
So, a vision of order they were bound to bless.

With democracy Germany had briefly flirted,
Which, to some, seemed just perverted,
As German people had been schooled,
In believing it best if a Kaiser ruled.

At first Britain watched with admiration,
Though some looked on with agitation,
When national socialism took a grip,
Of Germany's people and wouldn't slip.

Whilst at home, King George was more concerned,
With the large Labour Party which daily yearned,
For more reform and social improvement,
Gaining support for its radical movement.

Then nineteen twenty-six saw strikes,
As many labourers showed their dislikes,
Of how they were treated and paid a low wage,
With a general strike to show their rage.

Technology too was rapidly changing,
With inventions that were very wide ranging,
Including TV's and radio sets,
Which many embraced with few regrets.

The radio played an important part,
In people's lives from the start,
With BBC shows full of education,
The broadcasts welcomed without hesitation.

George had already spoken before,
On twenty third of April, nineteen twenty-four,
With his first Christmas broadcast in thirty-two,
Drawing an audience which only grew.

As the world changed, so decisions were made,
To ensure the old ideas would fade,
Ideas which saw Britain as the main focal point,
Of an empire which could its politicians appoint.

So, in nineteen thirty-one, after much debate,
Dominions were allowed to decide their fate,
As autonomous peoples, but still being part,
Of an equal empire with the king at its heart.

Yet this king was near to the end,
Which those around could not pretend,
Could be put off for much longer,
As George was ill and not getting stronger.

He'd been ill before, and had to give,
More work to his son that he might live,
But George wasn't happy as he'd heard,
Of the rich life led by Edward.

The stress of rule finally showed,
Failing health to the worries owed.
In January, nineteen thirty-six it failed,
With Edward, as king and Emperor hailed.

Edward VIII (1936)

Interesting Fact:

Edward came into conflict with the church because he wanted to marry the woman he loved, a divorcee, but the church disapproved of marriage after divorce, and Edward was supposed to be the head of the church.

Just a few weeks after his father was made,
King and Emperor plans were laid,
To see that Edward was invested,
As Prince of Wales as tradition suggested.

Yet his father had some serious doubts,
Because the prince's whereabouts,
Had been the cause of scandalous chat,
Of where the prince's morals sat.

For Edward liked to live and enjoy,
Life to the full, but that would annoy,
His father who was left alarmed,
As the royal reputation was harmed.

A series of scandalous love affairs,
Left people shocked and his father with cares,
Of how his son would be seen,
By those whose comments could be mean.

But Edward had helped his father when,

During the war he'd visit the men,

On different fronts and helped to raise,

The morale of the troops and received praise.

So, Edward's lust for what he craved,

Was seen as a prince who misbehaved,

Going against what his father required,

Because it was what Edward desired.

When his father died, some were concerned,

When protocols by Edward were spurned,

With parliament too feeling very guarded

When established conventions were disregarded.

Just a few months into his reign,

His disregard for the rules was plain,

When Edward proposed to a woman he'd met,

With his determination very soon set.

But the woman he chose had been divorced,

Her ex-husband lived so it wasn't endorsed,

By a parliament who said they couldn't belong,

To such an arrangement they thought to be wrong.

As head of the church, Edward had roles,

To defend the faith and their souls,

With the church's views on divorce very clear,

So, to wed a divorcee would be insincere.

But Edward wanted to do as he pleased,

With tension growing and not being eased,

By the fact the woman Edward had picked.

Was foreign, not noble, and the rules were strict.

The rules at the time strictly forbade,

The marriage and Edward could not evade,

The growing pressure for him to decide,

With so many against him and not on his side.

Edward knew he'd need to placate,
The constitution and so abdicate,
Leaving the throne for what he felt,
Was the hand of fate so cruelly dealt.

In December of nineteen thirty-six,
Due to his love and politics,
After only three hundred and twenty-six days,
King and nation went separate ways.

Yet Edward's love for the woman won through,
After all the attention and scandal, he drew,
With Wallace Simpson becoming, at last,
His wife which left the nation aghast.

But Edward's scandalous life wasn't finished,
His knack for trouble not yet diminished,
As this new Duke of Windsor went to see,
Hitler's regime in Germany.

As tensions in Europe began to rise,

Edward's tour came as a surprise,

As it showed just where his sympathies lay,

One more example of a prince gone astray.

George VI
(1936-1952)

Interesting Fact:

He suffered terribly with a bad speech impediment but took great steps to overcome it so he could address the nation via radio and give speeches when necessary.

Here was a prince who was not prepared,
To take the throne once his brother dared,
To abdicate for love and the life,
Which gave the freedom to choose his wife.

Prince Albert George was suddenly thrust,
Into the light and had to adjust,
To what the nation and empire expected,
Once he, by fate, had been selected.

A sickly child when he was young,
Prone to tears with a stammering tongue,
Left-handed by birth and with knock knees,
He wore splints and changed the hand to please.

For an education, the prince received,
One his parents truly believed,
Would be the best for his position,
As a naval cadet with its tradition.

He stayed in the navy and did his best,
To serve the ship but was hard pressed,
To fight the urge of being seasick,
Yet to his duty he would stick.

In World War one he would amaze,
When, at Jutland, he had praise,
Mentioned in dispatches when in command,
Of the turret gun which he manned.

Later, ill health would see him grieve,
As he was forced to sadly leave,
The navy, which was a place he knew,
Joining the Air Force where he flew.

After the war, he determined to marry,
The woman he loved, but who would parry,
All his proposals until at last,
Lady Elizabeth's reluctance passed.

But a life away from all the attention,
Believing his life wouldn't merit a mention,
Came to an end when his brother left,
Leaving Albert and all the empire bereft.

Many believed that the new King would fail,
Was weak and inept, sickly and pale,
With a terrible stammer that would impede,
Any ability to speak or lead.

Though George had taken steps to improve,
His stammering speech and so remove,
Much of the problem to allow him to speak,
To help remove the idea he was weak.

Albert chose a name to be called,
So, his critics might not be appalled,
Choosing George as it would restore,
The people's trust as it was before.

The coronation would take place,
At Westminster Abbey in the face,
Of television and radio stations,
Keen to show it all to the nations.

But not long after, disaster struck,
When once again war ran amok,
With peace in their time being undone,
With George's reign barely begun.

As the empire struggled with its own demise,
They'd watched German industry grow in size.
Whilst the British empire started to crack,
The German nation took a new tack.

For the thoughts of others, Germany didn't care,
As their industry grew and truth was rare.
A formidable force soon rose from the grave,
As their leader chose to play the knave.

The best British men from the very top,
Were sent to make the worries stop.
Trauma of war was suddenly remembered,
So, for the peace, pride was dismembered.

Appeasement and hope were soundly heeded,
So, the British Prime Minister talked and pleaded.
The Lion's heart was old and lame,
And, for a while, they could peace proclaim.

Giving them peace, for which people yearned,
When Chamberlain came home, the threat overturned,
They received that for which they'd longed,
And around their leader, they praised and thronged.

Jubilant in peace, their fears now allayed,
They never thought to be so betrayed.
For the German leader had a devious scheme,
A murderous and underlying theme.

Czechoslovakia, then Poland was invaded,
And German military might was paraded.
The empire's threats to declare its hostility,
Were received as a gesture of belated futility.

No promise to withdraw the troops had arrived,
So, again in a lifetime, war was contrived.
Once again, the Tommy donned his tin hat,
To face the machine gun's rat a tat tat.

So, the British took up their old position,
And given their same defiant mission:
Wait for the Hun their attack to deliver,
Then make the enemy shake and quiver.

But Germany had a new special trick,
That made her tactics efficient and slick.
Soon, the allies would learn their error,
As Germany delivered its brand-new terror.

Blitzkrieg stopped the old attrition,
Disrupting the allies' old disposition.
Piercing the lines with tanks and planes,
The German forces held the reins.

A war of movement based on the tank,
Destroyed resolve and morale soon sank.
The Tommies fought on in hamlet and wood,
Barely halting the enemy as they thought they should.

The planes overhead left them nervous and scared,
Then bombs and guns meant that no-one was spared.
Above the columns, the dive bomber roared,
Where the refugees ran, and the terror soared.

Churchill was chosen as their wartime leader,
A man who excelled as a public speaker.
Calls for peace, he quickly defied,
By reminding them all how Germany lied.

His words appealed to a nation, unsure,
Of what was to follow, how to endure.
His speeches inspired, would a nation enthrall,
Saying now was the time to give him their all.

The people of London showed their mettle,
And for anything but victory they wouldn't settle.
Together they stood and defiance hissed,
Hoping the Germans would get the gist.

With each new raid, the sky glowed red,
Yet British defiance still wouldn't shred.
Bombed and exhausted, at the end of their wits,
Soon they would call this the time of the Blitz.

Yet the king became loved and admired,
By the way he mingled and never tired,
Of meeting the people after a raid,
Ensuring their spirit would never fade.

George and Elizabeth would be seen,
Amongst the damaged battle scene,
Talking to people and listening to those,
Who'd barely escaped with a handful of clothes.

When Buckingham Palace too was hit,
The last of the critics had to admit,
That here was a king like no other,
Unlike his father and especially his brother.

Whilst fighting alone from the beginning,
The addition of allies gave hope to their winning.
The Americans and Russians were soon on her side,
And fighting together, they'd turn the tide.

Then came the war with imperial Japan,
So, the empire tried their advance to ban.
Yet colonies fell to the sun that had risen,
And many would languish in a Japanese prison.

The nation fought on all over the globe,

Its regalia of war it would not disrobe.

For the cause of freedom, Britain wouldn't refrain,

Then drew a line at El Alamein.

For Britain had chosen, in a trice,

Democracy should chance the fickle dice.

But she shelved all those freedoms that sweet liberty sends,

In the hope that her actions would justify ends.

Despite all her wealth and all good intentions,

She never lost her imperial pretensions.

But, two mighty allies had now come to the fore,

Whose strength and resources would win them the war.

When the war ended, the king appeared,

At Buckingham Palace where everyone cheered,

For he'd become their symbol of hope,

Their spirit of victory and will to cope.

Yet everyone knew the world had evolved,
With things which had to be resolved,
And the war had left survivor's minds altered,
So, the spirit of change never faltered.

The wartime government quickly lost,
To a Labour one who counted the cost,
Of what the empire had had to pay,
To keep totalitarian evils at bay.

The people wanted jobs and to see,
A healthier life with security,
So, the government promised a better tomorrow,
But from America they'd have to borrow.

The steps to commonwealth gathered speed,
With King and parliament seeing the need,
To make provision for those who saw,
The notion of empire had lost its draw.

The title of Emperor of India was dropped,
As the people there sought to adopt,
Independence and separate states,
Pakistan and India choosing their fates.

In nineteen forty-nine, the London Declaration,
Was the old empire's demonstration,
Of how the nations would proceed,
Which George, as head, would accede.

Though parts of the empire wanted to leave,
Not looking back or stopping to grieve,
Allowed to go in the spirit of choice,
As king and parliament heard their voice.

But the stress of war and change would lead,
To ill health and doctors would plead,
For George to show greater concern,
And not those warning signs to spurn.

Heavy smoking would also give,
A reduction in George's chance to live,
But he found the strength and will to attend,
The Festival of Britain which he'd commend.

As failing health made him weak,
With the outlook seeming bleak,
His daughter, Elizabeth, took on the part,
Of helper, ruler, and would details impart.

For she was the eldest child and so,
Would have the crown and need to show,
She could adjust and then illustrate,
Whether her rule would be bad or great.

In nineteen fifty-two King George had,
A heart condition which was bad,
Coronary thrombosis which would kill,
Leaving his body dead and still.

Elizabeth II
(1952-2022)

Interesting Fact:

Over the course of her lifetime, Elizabeth would be Queen of thirty-two sovereign states. Reigning for just over seventy years, she is the longest reigning monarch in British history, and the longest reigning female head of state in history.

Having received a good education,
Her father had the expectation,
Of knowing his daughter would have the role,
Of ruling and that would be her goal.

During the war, Elizabeth worked,
As a driver/mechanic, no duties shirked,
Showing the people, she was committed,
Her sense of duty by all admitted.

When hostilities ended, she had a plan,
To marry for love a nobleman,
Prince Philip whom she'd met before,
So, they were married after the war.

In nineteen forty-seven they wed,
But in the papers, it was said,
That because he had German connections,
There were many who had objections.

But Philip renounced all foreign ties,
Believing it to be very wise,
To cut himself off from what he knew,
Starting a whole different life anew.

For he and Elizabeth were from the start,
Much in love and they wouldn't part,
Being together for seventy years,
Despite the troubles and the tears.

Elizabeth didn't have long to wait,
Until she was carrying all the weight,
Of monarch when her father died,
A time when most of the people cried.

After a splendid coronation,
Filmed in colour for many a nation,
The Queen and Duke of Edinburgh sought,
To lead their lives as best they thought.

As head of the church and firm believer,
In God and that she was the receiver,
Of His blessings and His grace,
She gave her church a dignified face.

The Queen continued to help evolve,
The commonwealth states, and matters resolve,
Watching the nations develop and grow,
The ebb and tide of politics flow.

At home, she had to deal with a land,
Broken by war and whose life was bland,
Due to rationing which prevailed,
With luxury goods still curtailed.

The political world would rapidly change,
Both home and abroad in the exchange,
Of ideas and thoughts which were fed,
By TV and radio which everywhere sped.

Many prime ministers would come to her,
Newly elected and they would confer,
Discussing plans for the days to come,
Each minister beating his party's drum.

The Queen could also only look,
At all the decisions her people took,
Which they felt quickly improved,
Their lives but prewar values removed.

Mainly due to the post war boom,
In response to the previous gloom,
The people demanded peace and wealth,
Better education, better health.

The speed of change was very intense,
Which to her values made little sense,
With music, films, morality and more,
Changing and into old virtues tore.

Trying to give ministers some sound advice,
Which, she hoped, would suffice,
The Queen was like some great enclave,
Mostly untouched by a changing wave.

Yet a glimmer of what the future held,
Of what her line and marriage spelled,
Was seen when Charles, her son and heir,
Was made Prince of Wales in a grand affair.

Closer to home and even abroad,
The changing world could not be ignored,
With terrorist threats a real concern,
Not knowing where their sights would turn.

But even if the assassin intended,
To target the Queen, she was defended,
By a network of people and her forces,
Who wisely used all their resources.

An intruder did get into her room,
Though the Queen was calm and didn't fume,
Talking with the man who had dared,
To shock and inwardly leave her scared.

Yet, while the assassin to her hadn't struck,
One of her relatives ran out of luck,
Lord Mountbatten blown up and killed,
A political assassin's mission fulfilled.

And as politicians came and went,
Elizabeth's time would be spent,
Getting to know what they planned,
That she might better understand.

Prime ministers went and spoke with her,
Some of whom would incur,
A gentle rebuke or words of advice,
While the meeting was always cordial and nice.

Both Winston Churchill and Margaret Thatcher,
Politicians of such great stature,
Enjoyed her company over tea,
But not before they bent the knee.

And she was Queen when many events,
Like wars and shooting of presidents,
Fueled the flames of the people's outrage,
As more were able to judge and gauge.

When the Falklands War broke out,
There was never any doubt,
That she'd back her government's action,
But her son taking part caused worried distraction.

But scandal also came close to her door,
And the media circus stuck in its claw,
With first her sister Margaret showing,
In her a lust for life was growing.

Always one to see what she was missing,
Known for the men she was pictured kissing,
Margaret felt the system was flawed,
Keeping her back from the life she adored.

Yet the Queen, by people, was rarely blamed,
For family spirits which had to be tamed,
Seeing Elizabeth as a mother and queen,
A mother that many women had been.

Later, Charles, her son and heir
Married a lady, young and fair,
Lady Diana and the fairytale wedding,
Never showed where the marriage was heading.

For both were young and poorly suited,
Their compatibility soon disputed,
And when Diana won heart and mind,
Cracks in the marriage weren't hard to find.

When seen together, the people displayed,
Such love for Diana it left Charles afraid,
That in her light the world couldn't see,
The sort of prince he wanted to be.

The Prince of Wales had duly found,
He walked upon uncertain ground,
Where he was lost in Diana's light,
Which, to the people, burned so bright.

It didn't help that their marriage was strained,
Because his love for another remained,
Camilla, a married woman who,
Understood Charles and whose love was true.

In time Diana and Charles would split,
Each of them thinking the other unfit,
To understand what the other desired,
With accusations leaving the nation tired.

Diana believed she did not belong,

In a system which treated her so wrong,

And when she died in a bad car crash,

Royal prestige was what the media would trash.

Throughout this storm, the Queen was hurt,

By all the scandal and the dirt,

Which the media sought and revealed,

As such dirty scandal to many appealed.

But Elizabeth always met the disgrace,

With dignity and there was never a trace,

Of what her feelings truly were,

As she tried to ignore the pain and the slur.

In nineteen ninety-two there struck,

Disasters which were just bad luck,

From a fire to photographs being produced,

With the Queen's morale being reduced.

Though Elizabeth knew what was expected,
Knew that she, by God, was selected,
To carry on with the business at hand,
Meeting and greeting as the government planned.

Meeting the foreign leaders became,
One of the reasons she acquired such fame,
As some were seen as wise and just,
While others were known for greed and lust.

Yet Elizabeth met with good and bad,
Both from the free world and those who had,
Ruled their lands with an iron fist,
Though her demeanour would persist.

She went abroad and was invited,
To meet foreign leaders who were delighted,
To meet the Queen who was entertained,
With great respect for her maintained.

Whatever the country it didn't matter,
As crowds would gather to watch and chatter,
About the Queen, who'd wave and smile,
Full of royal pomp and style.

As the years passed the love and affection,
For Elizabeth grew and upon reflection,
The people of Britain knew they cherished,
Their queen with a love which hadn't perished.

On Christmas day, most people sat,
In front of TV's with Christmas hat,
To watch her speak and wish all well,
Enchanted by her majestic spell.

So, when the time came to celebrate,
Her years on the throne they would create,
Such special shows and great displays,
Which were seen as wonderful days.

Silver, golden, diamond and platinum,
The nation celebrated to the maximum,
Showing their love and affection for,
Their Queen who was at Britain's core.

Towards the end, the Queen oversaw,
A hot debate which left people raw,
When the government left an important decision,
To the people and caused a great division.

The nation was asked to make a choice,
Given the chance to have a voice,
On the European Union and if to stay,
Or throw its membership away.

Elizabeth watched as the people debated,
Heard how the membership was loved and hated,
Until the day came when the people voted,
Decided to leave, and victors then gloated.

A few years later, the world had to face,
A major illness in the human race,
When from the east, like the plague before,
Came Covid-19 to everyone's door.

Yet the Queen was there for all to see,
Wearing her mask and PPE,
For many a comfort in a world under threat,
Showing her dignity as each crisis was met.

In twenty twenty-one, she lost her prince,
Philip who'd been with her ever since,
Their marriage seventy-three years before,
His loss a harsh and painful sore.

Then, a year later, in twenty twenty-two,
After her jubilee, concerns for her grew,
As the Queen was ill and things looked bleak,
For Elizabeth was very old and weak.

On the eighth of September, frail and thin,
Her body and mind finally gave in,
Closing her eyes and falling asleep,
Leaving a loving world to weep.

For seventy years, the Queen represented,
A reign which was almost unprecedented,
The longest a woman was ever seated,
Upon the throne and so warmly greeted.

For Elizabeth truly liked to engage,
With people regardless of race or age,
Listening to the stories which they had,
And her death, to many, was tragic and sad.

Charles III (2022-)

Interesting Fact:

With a very keen interest in architecture, Charles supports the preservation of historic buildings, and is a great supporter of charities, becoming the patron or president of more than eight hundred charities and organisations.

Of all the princes that have waited,
For the throne and felt frustrated,
Charles's wait was the longest known,
With some believing his chance had flown.

Despite the length of his mother's life,
Her reign and all his personal strife,
The title of King was eventually gained,
For which the prince was suitably trained.

His first act was to give a speech,
Hoping he would the nation reach,
To help reassure and give comfort to,
A people who mourned the queen they knew.

Yet Charles was never afraid to say,
What he believed or how to display,
The beliefs he held so very dear,
Often making his opinions clear.

His personal life had attracted attention,
Causing his family apprehension,
As the media circus always looked,
For truth or lies or whatever was cooked.

His turbulent marriage to Diana had,
Left an image of him which was bad,
As he was seen as the man who'd forced,
The people's love to being divorced.

Rightly or wrongly, opinions stuck,
With the media always slinging the muck,
With fingers at Charles constantly pointed,
With love for Diana, the people's anointed.

In love at first, or so they'd appear,
The nation's affection seemed to be clear,
And when the Princess gave birth to a boy,
The world reacted with praise and joy.

Though his secret love for another revealed,
This was the story which really appealed,
To a nation hungry for dirt and gossip,
Juicy tales to be heard on each lip.

But Charles had feelings and a sensitive side,
Which many would mock and even deride,
Seeing their prince as being too soft,
So, words of derision to him would waft.

During an interview the nation was told,
That his parents to him seemed very cold,
And when at school, he was bullied and shamed,
His father, Prince Phillip, was partially blamed.

Yet Charles was not to be anyone's fool,
Had shown his intelligence even at school,
Displaying an interest in modern things,
Unlike so many of Britain's Kings.

After this he served in the armed forces,
Attending all the necessary courses,
To become a pilot then went to sea,
To serve, like his father, in the Royal Navy.

Charles could see how the world was going,
How new ideas were overflowing,
Making things change at a rapid pace,
And Charles desired to be part of the race.

From early on, his great inclination,
Was toward ideas and innovation,
Enjoying his time discussing with those,
Who took the time to talk and disclose.

His charitable work has helped improve,
The lives of many and helped remove,
Many comments and any doubt
Of what the King cares much about.

His love of historic buildings meant,
A message to all the nation was sent,
In which the King has clearly stated,
His time and effort will be donated.

He is the oldest to attain,
The throne of Britain in that chain,
Of Kings and Queens which stretches through,
Time and place where tradition grew.

On a cold and very wet day,
Charles went forth with much display,
To have the crown put on his head,
As by tradition he was led.

His wife Camilla was by his side,
Whose presence Charles would not hide,
For he insisted she would be Queen,
Crowned with him that love was seen.

Together in their magnificent coach,
Where only servants might approach,
Charles and Camilla, in royal attire,
Their image lifted ever higher.

At Westminster Abbey, the world was shown,
How British tradition has lasted and grown,
As Charles and Camilla were anointed and crowned,
With all the pomp and majestic sound.

And while some say it's out of date,
That monarchs should not lead the state,
Charles showed he was in tune with those,
Who might speak out and oppose.

A modern king with his own ideas,
A sensitive man with passion and fears,
Who'll rule the nation and do his best,
To set an example and pass the test.

Other Books by the author:

Republic to Empire to Chaos (the Roman Empire)

Faith, War & Disease (the Middle Ages)

The Tudors

The English Civil War

Scores to Settle (WW1)

World War 2

Britain Through the Ages

A History of the USA

Living in the Past

Printed in Great Britain
by Amazon